A COUNTRY ESCAPE

KM Publishing

BY KM LOWE

Bio

Author History

Kelly McMullen Lowe was born on the 19th of March, 1986 to the proud parents of Christine Greenlees Beaumont Steedman and Hugh Patrick McMullen. My parents taught me the true value of life and they showed me how to succeed. I married my husband David Lowe, on the 30th of December, 2006. We have two wonderful children named Dylan and Tianna. Over the last couple of years, I have been unwell and I put all my time into my family and reading. In 2012, I wanted to commit myself to writing my own novel. I have put a lot of time and effort into all of my books. I hope that you enjoy them, as much I did writing them.

Acknowledgements

First of all, I would like to thank Zee at ZH Designs, for helping me to create a beautiful cover for my fifth novel. You have helped me through a difficult time when I couldn't find what I was looking for. I will always be grateful to you for your help with my cover and street team.

Secondly, I would like to thank Alan Riehl, for editing my books. This process has been so much easier with you on my side. You answered all of my questions. I hope to have you as my editor for a long time to come.

In addition, I would like to thank my family and friends for putting up with me over the last couple of years. My husband will get some sense out of me for a couple of weeks, until I start writing again. This book would not have been possible, if it wasn't for the support of my husband. I love you to the moon and back.

Next, I would like to thank my children for being my little angels. I love you dearly and you mean the world to me. I hope that one day you will be able to read mummy's work. In the meantime, Dylan, you can read the blurb. My son is my very own bookworm. I hope when he gets older, he will still enjoy reading.

Finally to my readers. Thank you all, for purchasing my books. It means a lot to see so many of you reading what I write. All of your lovely reviews and comments make everything worthwhile. Your buying The Beautiful Life Trilogy gave me the spark I needed when I was at a low point in my life. I have made many new friends from all over the world. That wouldn't have been possible, if it wasn't for my writing. I would like to thank everyone on my street team. Without Suzie and the other ladies, I would be snowed under with promoting books. You ladies take a lot of the pressure off of me and that allows me to keep writing.

Thank you

Dedications

I would like to dedicate this novel to my wonderful husband, David. He isn't just my husband. He is my best friend. He has shown me so much support over the last couple of years and I can't thank him enough.

We have been through some difficult times lately, but together we have gotten through everything together. There might have been tears and tantrums, but having each other for support, was all we needed to face another day.

Chapter 1

A Country Escape

Molly

Looking out around the acres of land that comes along with this property, gives me a sense of freedom. I've always been used to a fast paced city life, but this move to the country could be just what I need. It could be the move that helps me make the most out of life.

It is either a make or break move that I need to do, in order to get my life back on track.

"Miss McGregor? Have you seen enough of the property?" I turned around slowly to see the middle-aged man stop a few feet away from me, with his expensive leather brief case dangling beside him. Under any ordinary circumstances, I would normally stay clear of this type of man, because I can't deal with people looking down their noses at others. We all entered the world the same way and we will all leave the same way. I just don't agree with others thinking that they are better, all because they have a good job and plenty of money in the bank. As hard as it was, I had to put my thoughts and feelings aside and smile brightly at this man.

I was here to see a potential property that I could spend the rest of my life with. I wasn't here to judge the estate agent in front of me, no matter how he made me feel.

"Please, call me Molly. I have seen more than enough. I'll get my solicitor to place an offer when I get back."

I knew what I wanted and there was nothing else to it. I love the country air that surrounded me and I feel free. I just love the property so much that I could move in right now.

It was going to be mine if I got my way. Maybe just this once, luck was on my side for a change.

"Great! If your partner wants to view the property, then we can arrange for that to happen," he said, nonchalantly, like he knew me.

I let out a little snigger before I corrected his arrogant arse. "It is just me that is moving out here, so that won’t be necessary."

I watched his mouth drop open slightly. I wondered why he was so shocked. Did only married couples buy property in the country?

"Oh, I am sorry, Molly. I just assumed." I watched his eye's roam down to my swollen tummy and I felt like telling him it was rude to assume. Especially when he couldn't be further from the truth.

I placed my hand over my tummy protectively and smiled brightly at the man in front of me. "To set the record straight, it is just me and my three dogs moving up here, that's if my offer is accepted. I wanted to relocate my business somewhere quiet for when the baby arrives." I tried to bite my tongue and keep back any sarcastic responses.

"I am sorry. I didn't mean to offend you." So he said, but I didn't seem convinced by his apology.

"Oh you didn't, Mr. Leroy. I guess I had better get used to everyone knowing my business. Isn't that what happens in small country villages?" I know what I've read in books and watched in films, so I am prepared for the tittle-tattle. I'm going to be the new pregnant girl in town. I am looking forward to seeing what assumptions the other villagers come up with. I will be the gossip until something else takes their attention.

"I guess so, my dear," he said quietly, as if someone stole his tongue all of a sudden. It is a pity he wasn't as quiet at the beginning. Maybe we wouldn't have gotten off on the wrong foot.

"Well, if that's everything for now, I'll let you get on. I'm sure you have a lot on today." I didn't mean to sound so unsociable, but I really hated people that saw a pregnant woman and assumed all sorts. I mean, really? It is the 21st century that we live in now. Kids have kids these days.

"Of course, Molly. The previous owners are selling due to their parents passing. Just between us, they are looking for a quick sale. I've had a few viewings this week but no offers as of yet." I was waiting for the scare tactics. My father did say he would use this line on me.

"Let's just hope it stays that way until I phone my solicitor. I don't think I could cope if I wasn't quick enough. Everything is all organized at my end, or as organized as it can be. I've just been looking for the perfect property to come along. My dad has been keeping his eyes and ears open for me, for some time now. When he told me about this property in Throsk, outside of Stirling, I immediately fell in love with all the pictures. I've shopped a lot in Stirling over the years, but I didn't realize that a village like this existed." I realized that I just rambled on, but he did the dutiful thing and listened to me.

When I am excited about something, I can't seem to stop myself from talking. I have been like that since I was a child. My mum and dad would laugh at me when I spoke ninety miles an hour.

"You are still close enough to everything, but far enough away from the hustle and bustle of the city life." I could only nod at the estate agent as I imagined my life here. I had to rein in my thoughts, because I was getting distracted by taking in the scenery.

"I can picture myself living here, so if you can, please put other buyers off." Both the estate agent and myself shared a gentle laugh together, as we walked back toward our cars. I know I probably sounded desperate, but I didn't care now. I wanted to be settled for the baby's arrival and this location was perfect. I was beginning to think that I would take anything that came along in the end, because time was starting to run out for me. This was just a bit of luck.

"I'll do my best, Molly. Please act quickly if you really want this to be yours."

"Don't worry, Mr. Leroy. I'm heading back to my bed and breakfast just outside Fallin. I'll call my solicitor right away. Thank you for your time." Our attitude had both changed toward each other and we were both more at ease. I just wished that the rest of the appointment was as laid back as the last five minutes.

"Take care, Molly." As much as I didn't want to shake his hand, I felt a sudden surge of excitement. I was going to forget about his arrogance at the beginning of our meeting. I extended my hand out to him, while I kept one hand protectively on my small bump. It was amazing how protective I felt over my unborn child.

"Bye for now, Mr. Leroy," I said, as a matter of urgency.

I had to get back quickly. I had to get things moving before someone else snatched this property from under me. If I had anything to do with it, then that wasn't going to happen.

"Bye, Molly," he said, as he placed his briefcase in the boot of his car.

I quickly walked back to my own car watching my footing on the uneven ground, because I was clumsy at the best of times, never mind when I'm excited and not thinking clearly. The growing bump in front of me was also stopping me from seeing my feet.

I sat in my car and rested my head on the headrest. It was unbelievably crazy how I was moving away from everything I've ever known. I was born and bred in Aberdeen, but since I found out I was pregnant, I wanted a new life. I run a rescue shelter for dogs back home and I was so proud of myself for starting from scratch. After I graduated with my degree in Veterinary Medicine, I knew exactly what path I wanted to take. I had everything all set in my mind and I just went for it. My life was looking so positive and I was happy now that I could see a clear picture of my future.

I had been dating Bradley for two years. We met at university, but it wasn't until a week before graduation that we went on a date with one another. He was ruggedly handsome and he swept me off my feet. Thinking about it now, I have no idea how we lasted so long. We had two years of ups and downs, but when I found out about the baby, he finished things and told me to go for an abortion. Of course, that was never going to happen. After my brother Grey showed him his fists, I never saw or heard from him again.

I keep telling myself that I had a lucky escape. Who knows where my life would have ended up if we kept going the way we were. Now I know why people say mental exhaustion is worse than physical exhaustion, because I was dead on my feet trying to keep him with me all the time. When I think back to our time together, I felt stupid for putting up with him for so long.

The only thing that I care about now, is my unborn child and my dogs. This country escape is just what we all need.

***

"How did your viewing go, hen?" I was just through the front door to my bed and breakfast, when the landlady, Sylvia bounced toward me looking for all the details. Her small chubby frame makes her look and feel like a warm motherly figure. We connected with one another the moment I walked through her door.

"Well..." I couldn't help but keep her in suspense, because I knew how excited she was for me.

For anyone that walked in here and didn't know us, they would think we were family.

I've only been here a day but we hit it off immediately. She practically made me eat all of her homemade cooking last night while we spoke. I must have eaten my body weight in food. We somehow managed to forget about the time and talked for hours.

"You'll find somewhere soon sweetheart. Don’t give up." Her voice toned down and I could immediately see how much she wanted this for me.

"I loved it, Sylvia!" I shrieked with excitement.

I was beyond excited now and I couldn't hide it from a single soul. I wanted the whole world to know how excited I was.

" Come through and I'll get us some tea and shortbread. I want to hear all about it and don't you dare leave out any details!" Sylvia took my hand and I followed her through to the small lounge. "Sit down and make yourself comfortable. I'll be right back."

I don't know who was more excited, me or Sylvia. I just knew we were going to speak about it until we had nothing else left to say.

I watched Sylvia walk through to the kitchen, as I took off my jacket and sat down on her nice comfy couch. I feel so comfortable here. That certainly isn't like me in strange surroundings, so I took that as a good sign.

I arrived yesterday afternoon. The moment I met Sylvia, she instantly became a mother figure to me. We stayed up until way after midnight chatting away. I told her all about my life and I listened to her telling me about hers. It felt nice being here. So warm and welcoming.

"Here we go, my darling. Now, do tell me all about it." Sylvia clapped her hands together the moment she placed the tray down.

"I'll give you the brief details, but I need to call my solicitor. I'm sure we will talk about it until the wee hours," I explained.

"That must be a good thing that you're keen to phone your solicitor. You're not going to sleep on it before you make your decision? You must be sure," said Sylvia, softly, as she handed me the mug of tea. I couldn't stop smiling, because she has made me so much tea since I arrived here, that she can remember exactly what I take. My own brother doesn't know what I take in my tea.

"I know you love my tea, but don't keep me in suspense. I am old if you haven't noticed and my heart can't take it any longer," she joked.

"Well, apart from the estate agent being an arrogant prick to start off with, it all turned out great. Obviously, a lot of work will need to be done to get the house brought into this century. The conversion of the barns will take a little while, but I see myself there. I've got the money behind me to do it and now seems like the right time for me to make this change." I felt like I was trying to convince myself that this was the right thing to do, because I have always had to answer to my family. However, sitting here with Sylvia has made me realize that I don't have anyone to convince. This is my life and I am going to start living it.

“I hope you gave that old bugger what for." Sylvia moved in to engage in conversation with me, with that smirk on her face. I had a funny feeling that I knew exactly what she would have said to my arrogant estate agent had she been there with me. She did warn me that he might see a young woman and then try his luck at pressuring me into buying.

"It's funny, because I don't know where my confidence came from but I had all the right answers for him. For the first time in my life I didn't feel pressured or bullied. I made my mind up the moment I set eyes on him, that I wasn't going to stand for his arrogance. I gave him just as good as he gave me, if not more.”

"That's my girl," said Sylvia, as she sipped on her tea. "So, are we going to be seeing more of you around here?" I looked into my cup while I felt a smile spread across my face.

" I'm going to put an offer in just as soon as my tea is finished. Oh, Sylvia! I really want this! I can just picture myself there with the baby on my doorstep. No travelling.

No rental fees for the shelter. Everything is just perfect." Just hearing my words aloud, made me feel all giddy. I felt like it was all too good to be true though.

"I love talking to you, but what are you waiting for? Give me that cup, get up to your room, and make the call! I can make us tea at any time of day." I giggled at Sylvia, because she wasn't like a regular old person. She was the cool granny that everyone wanted. "Go!"

"I'm going! I'm going!" I got up and grabbed my bag and jacket while heading to my room. "Wish me luck," I shouted back to Sylvia, as I left her sitting in the lounge.

"You don't need any luck! I can feel it in my water!" she shouted back at me.

If anyone heard us, they would think we were crazy shouting odd things back and forward to each other. It felt nice to be here with someone like Sylvia. Out of the whole area, I had to find Sylvia's B&B. I think that was my first sign that this was the right move for me.

I still expect someone to come and snatch it all away from me before it has even started. However, I somehow hoped and prayed that Sylvia was right. I know older people usually have a six sense, but I couldn't quite believe that ever happens. I am not very superstitious but I wanted to believe that she was right.

I reached my nice cozy room and slumped down on the bed putting my feet up. I might only be twenty weeks pregnant, but my body and feet are beginning to ache. I was just a little too excited to care about my aches and pains right now.

I leaned forward and grabbed my phone from my bag. I couldn't wait a moment longer to phone my solicitor. I quickly hit his number and hoped there was an answer.

I looked at my watch and realized it was noon. A lot of people take late lunches, but I was relieved when the ring tone stopped and a lady's soft voice answered my call. "Hello. You're through to Jacob Jones' line. How can I help you?"

I gave myself a soft shake and realized I needed to speak before the line went dead. "Hello. This is Molly McGregor. Mr. Jones has been waiting for my call. It is regarding a property I was just viewing." I tried to give her all the information she may need to process my call, without it taking too long.

"Okay. Hold the line, please," said the lady on the phone, who I imagined was some secretary or personal assistant for Jacob Jones.

I had the soft classical music playing, as I sat on hold. I realized it must have only been a few minutes, but it felt like a spell had been cast and time had suddenly stopped.

The music made me nervous. My hands were sweaty. My heart was racing. I just wanted the call to end already.

"Sorry for your wait, Miss McGregor. I will transfer your call straight away."

"Th...thank you." I stuttered, because I was too used to the sound of classical music.

If I thought I was nervous before, then that was nothing compared to right at this moment. My nerves had kicked in full speed and I was feeling sick as a pig. I just want to get my offer in and get my hands on the keys. That wasn't so much to ask. Was it?

"Molly. It's good to hear from you. How has your country trip been?" Jacob Jones. Finally.

"Good. In fact, it is perfect. I want to put the asking price in for Ethel's Farm in Throsk. I've fallen head over heels in love with it, Jacob. It is perfect for everything I want and need."

"Really? You do know that you can get the price down a few grand." I knew that he was going to tell me all of this, but I didn't want to take any chances. I knew what I wanted and I wasn't going into any bidding wars with anyone.

"I know, but I'm taking no chances. I want to move in as soon as possible. Unless you haven't noticed, I am five months pregnant. I don't have time to banter with them. It's now or never." I stated clearly my intentions, because I wasn't going to be talked around. I knew what I wanted.

"Okay. I'll take care of everything for you. You'll hear from me as soon as I know something. Unless a bid has been accepted, I can't see them turning it down."

"Thank you, Jacob. Mr. Leroy did say that they had a few viewings last week, but nothing came of them," I explained.

"Molly..."

"Yeah?" I answered quickly, because I was worried to see where this was going.

"I've known you from the beginning of your adult life. I take care of all your legal business and I will always follow your orders..."

I sensed a *but* coming and the silence made me nervous. "You do want this. Don't you? I mean, once the deal is done you're going to be stuck with it for a long time." I actually felt a bit pissed off, because I wondered why he felt the need to question my decision.

"I appreciate your concern Jacob, I really do, but I've thought about this long and hard. I've been waiting for an opportunity like this for so long. Who would have thought a screwed up relationship and an unplanned pregnancy would make me see what I want in life? This farm is perfect for me. For business and pleasure," I sighed with relief when I finally stopped talking.

"Okay. You sound sure," he said, sounding defeated by my come back.

"I am. I've never been more certain about anything in my entire life."

"Great! Leave it with me."

"Thank you, Jacob," I said, feeling excited that I'd got through the hard part of this next step.

"Take care, Molly. I'll be in touch."

"Bye," I said, even quicker this time, as I threw my phone down beside me on the bed.

I was getting so fed up of answering the same questions. I think they all forget that I am an adult now. Even my dad didn't give me as much grief. He was on my side from the beginning and he was looking forward to my fresh start more than I was.

I left my dad back home waiting for the daily updates. I love my father dearly and I know that it must be very difficult for him to watch me move down here to the country. Especially, while I have a baby on the way with no partner for support. I guess he had every reason to worry, because I don't always go by the rulebook. If there is a hard way to do something, then I generally do it that way.

I did half expect my dad to go ballistic when he found out about the baby, but he showed me nothing but love and support. It was a lot more than I could ask for.

My dad can always read people like a book and I went against his warnings about Bradley. He seemed to see through his nice features. I guess the saying, love is blind, is very true.

I gave myself a shake and pulled up the throw from the bottom of the bed. I had to stop thinking about everyone else and concentrate on what the baby needs. The only thing he or she needs right now, is rest.

I suddenly feel exhausted after all of today's excitement. This was one thing that I won't miss when the baby is born. Sleepy brain. I just have to sit down and I feel tired all the time. I guess I should get as much sleep as I can before the baby does arrive. Going with what people have told me, I won’t be getting much sleep over the next couple of years.

Before I know it, it will be dirty nappies and sleepless nights.

***

"Molly! Molly!" shouted Sylvia.

I thought I had been dreaming when I woke up from my nap, so I turned onto my back and tried to compose myself. I felt like I could carry on sleeping.

"Molly, my dear? Are you okay?" came a soft voice with a tap on my door.

I quickly realized I hadn't been dreaming and I stumbled up to open my room door. I felt dazed and wobbly on my feet.

"Molly? Are you okay?" asked Sylvia, concerned.

"Sorry. I must have fallen asleep after I spoke with my solicitor," I said, as I reached over and flicked on the light switch.

"You had me worried when you didn't show for dinner." I looked at her funny, because I felt like I had just lost a day.

"Really? What time is it?" I asked, now curious of how long I'd been sleeping.

"It's passed eight, hen. You really must have needed your rest. You've had a busy couple of days."

"I must have been tired. I can't remember the last time I slept like that during the day."

"I can remember the tired stages of pregnancy, so I left you some dinner in the microwave." I couldn't help but smile at Sylvia as she patted my arm affectionately.

"What would I do without you, Sylvia?" She's really looked after me since my arrival.

"I'm heading to my quarters, if you need me. Make yourself at home in the kitchen. I've left you scones and cakes on the table in the container."

"Thank you and good night, Sylvia." I know I was pregnant, but by the time I left Sylvia's B&B, I was going to be the size of a house.

"Aye. You too, hen. I hope you can sleep after your long nap."

"Tell me about it." I laughed, as I closed the door behind Sylvia. Although I had slept for several hours, I had a funny feeling that I would find sleep very easy after I had something to eat.

My plan for tomorrow is to make myself busy during the day, because whenever I sit down I want to sleep. My get up and go has left me, but I aimed to get it back. If I get all my plans in place and try to get all the paper work sorted, then I will feel more at ease.

It is a waiting game and patience isn't my strong point.

Chapter 2

A Life On The Farm

Greg

Rushing around at this time of morning was a pain in my arse. Every morning it was the same routine. Up at 4:30 to start the morning jobs on the farm. My poor mother would come over and watch Kayleigh for me while I worked. I would come back to my cottage by 7:00 to get Kayleigh up for showers and breakfast. This is the hardest job of the morning.

"I would love it if one morning that little witch would get out of that bed, first time. I am sure she does it just to get on my nerves." I laugh, as I entered my kitchen where my mum has breakfast cooked for me and Kayleigh.

"You know, Greg. She is just like you were as a child." My mum's small frame leans against my kitchen worktop, as I scowl in her direction making her giggle.

"Did I get better as I got older?"

"Eh...No! I had to threaten you with cold water many mornings. I can remember when you had your first girlfriend. You were up, showered, breakfast, teeth brushed, and out the door waiting for the bus, before I even had the chance to tell you what to do."

I couldn't stop rolling my eyes as I heard my mum talk about my younger years. I'm sure she takes great pleasure in reminding me about things I clearly want to forget.

"You know. It wouldn't do you any harm to go out once in a while to find someone to have some fun with."

"Mum..." I sit down on the chair and stretch my legs out in front of me, while running my hands through my hair. "I don't have the time for a relationship. I have a daughter who enjoys taking the piss out of me. I have a business and a farm to run. I work from 4:30 in the morning to 5 every night. Then I come in to look after Missy. Can you tell me where my schedule would fit around going out and having fun?"

"You're young, Greg. Don't...I'll say this to you again, before you walk off and leave me talking to myself. Don't cut yourself off from love, because of previous experiences. I know you might not like to hear this, but you got your daughter from previous experiences so it isn't all bad."

I stand up and rinse my cup out before placing it in the dishwasher. I know that my mum means well, but I'm not interested in any of this now. I have bigger fish to fry and none of those fish include getting a woman.

"A life on the farm doesn't mean you can't love or be loved." I got to the doorframe of my kitchen and turn to see my mum at the dishwasher.

I understand what she means. I understand that she wants to see me happy in love, but that ship sailed a long time ago. Now I have the only thing I need. My daughter.

I got outside and let the cold air hit my face. As much as some mornings I hate the early rises, the moment I come outside I know where I truly belong.

“Greg! We have a sick cow in the east barn. Can you call a vet before you come out?” my brother asks, as he stops in front of my house.

“Aye. No bother.”

“I have put it in quarantine until we know what’s wrong.”

“Great! I’ll be out in five minutes.” I take a deep breath and enter my house again to make the phone call. There is never a quiet day on the farm and always something crops up to make the day unique.

Never a dull moment.

Chapter 3

Good News

Molly

The waiting game begins. Rather than explore the local area, I decide to use the peace and quiet to my advantage. After breakfast, Sylvia and her housekeeper are busy cleaning and getting ready to face another day.

Meanwhile, I open my laptop and decide to search for local builders and joiners. Although the farmhouse is clean, it is going to need some work done. To get it to my liking, it is going to need a lot of work. The barns need a conversion so I can re-launch my animal shelter. The gardens and surrounding land needs a lot of TLC, but it will all be perfect when it is finished. I need to remember that *Rome wasn't built in a day.*

I know I have a lot of work ahead of me, but I've never been afraid of hard work. I was always brought up with a level head on my shoulders. My dad was a firm believer that what's for you won't go by you. In order to get what you want in life, you have to work hard. This was one piece of advice that I always listened to.

I certainly don't cut corners. I'm not letting my pregnancy stop me from doing this. I keep telling everyone that I am pregnant, not ill. It doesn't stop them from fussing over me. Anyone would think I was fragile like a porcelain doll, the way my family treats me.

"You have been glued to that screen all morning. Your eyes are going to end up square," said Sylvia, placing fresh tea and biscuits down beside me.

"Thank you, Sylvia."

I have never been in a bed and breakfast before, where I have felt so comfortable and at home. Usually, I would lock myself away in my room for the entire stay, but I am happy to come down and sit in the lounge or the dining room.

"You really need to keep your strength up, young lady." Here comes the motherly tone of concern.

"This is the easy bit. I am just looking through local builders and joiners," I explained.

I watched Sylvia pull the seat out beside me and sit down. "I know. I know. I'm getting ahead of myself and getting my hopes up, but I can't help it. I know this house is meant to be mine, Sylvia."

"I was only going to say, that you don't need to look too far." I raised my brows in Sylvia's direction, as I took a sip of my tea.

"You know someone?" I was getting excited, as I interrupted her.

"Macintosh's farm is right next door to you. Mr. and Mrs. Macintosh live there but their two sons run the show. They're both battling their health problems."

"So, their sons are into the building trade?" I asked.

"Gregor is the oldest. He was a city boy after graduating with an architect's degree. Two years ago when his old man had a heart attack, he had to come home. He agreed that he would help his young brother Sam, run the family business. We all call upon the boys if we need any building or maintenance work done."

I couldn't believe that I was hearing all of this after my morning of searching the wonderful world of internet.

"Don't you think I'll have too much work for just two men?" I really don't know anything about the building trades, so I realize that I would probably say something stupid.

"Don't be silly. Gregor runs his own business from the farm. He has a team of men that do the building work. Occasionally, if the jobs are too big, Gregor steps in. You should get in touch with him, because he could give you a quote. Tell him I sent you."

"I don't want to jump in with both feet too soon, until I wait to hear back from my solicitor. If nothing happens by Sunday, then I need to go home."

I instantly felt sad saying that, because already this felt like home. I feel like my feet were under the table and I never want to leave.

"No news is good news, hen."

"So they say," I said gloomy, as I sip away at my nice hot tea.

"What do you have planned for this afternoon?" she asked, cheerily.

"I'm going to go for a walk. Clear my head." I hated to be stuck in my own thoughts. If I stayed glued to this computer, then that's exactly what will happen.

"Don't go too far and take your phone!" exclaimed my mother hen.

"Yes ma'am." I laughed, as I packed my things up from the table. I've waited so long to have someone like Sylvia back in my life.

"I just care about my guests." I look down into Sylvia's eyes and can see that she is at her happiest when she is looking after someone.

" I appreciate everything you've done for me," I say, placing my hand over Sylvia's small warm hand. "I love your fussing."

It's nice to know that if I get this property, then I will have someone that I can turn to for a friendly chat. That is one thing I'm dreading about moving to a new place. I am never good at mingling with strangers. I always wait until someone approaches me.

Since I lost my mum last year, I've felt like a little piece of my life is missing. However, since I've been here with Sylvia, I've felt like I am in the right place. Even if I don't get this property, I'll wait until another property in this area comes on the market.

Thinking about my mum and Sylvia, they are like two peas in a pod. My mum would have told me exactly what Sylvia has. Now I know I am on the right path. It is like my guardian angel has sent me here to this property.

It has been waiting for me all along.

"I'll only be out for a little while. I'll be back for lunch if you fancy showing me somewhere nice to eat."

"It's a date. My new guests aren't arriving until 5, so I'll have some time to spare when all the chores are done."

I can't stop smiling at Sylvia. It's like I gave her a million pounds asking her to come for lunch with me. I bet she doesn't get much company outside of her bed and breakfast.

"Great!" I yelled a little too excited. "I'll put all of this away before I get my hiking boots on."

I now had a good afternoon in front of me.

A good start to beating the pregnancy blues.

***

Before I left the B&B, Sylvia made sure I had water in my bag. I laughed at first, because it was dull and over cast when I left, but within an hour of me walking, the sun was splitting the trees. I saw a cut down tree stump just up ahead at the end of a country road, so I made my way to get a seat for five minutes while I recovered from my trek. It's amazing how tiring it is carrying a little bump around with me.

It's hard to believe that I could be living amongst all of this beautiful scenery at some point. Everything is gorgeous.

I just want my phone to ring to put me out of my misery. One way or another. The waiting is what's killing me. I have never been good at waiting around for something to happen.

Suddenly, a large black Labrador jumps up at me out of nowhere. I am showered with kisses and plenty of affection by the large dog.

"Hiya, gorgeous," I say, in a funny tone, as I scratch her floppy ears and let her kiss me.

"Mia! Come here girl! You're a very bad girl!" There is this tall, muscular man bending down and placing her lead on. "I am so sorry. She didn't hurt you. Did she?" I fussed around the over excited dog.

"Sorry. No, she never hurt me at all. She only wanted to say *hello*." I take my attention back off the man and show the dog that I am still talking to her as well.

"I take her in the fields with me, but the first person or animal she snaps her eyes on, she is off like a shot." I giggle at this silly dog in front of me and I have no idea why.

"She is gorgeous," I say, never looking up at the man.

"I'm sorry if this sounds rude of me. Are you okay?" He bends down to my level, blushing beetroot red.

"I'm fine. I'm staying at the B&B along the road. I'm just out exploring the area, because I've just put an offer in for Ethel's Farm."

Silent hit him and I look up to see him with a surprised look on his face.

"So, we could be neighbors at some point." He manages to snap out of his silent trance to talk to me.

"I guess so. If you live around here."

"You must think I got my manners from a lucky bag. I am Gregor, but you can call me Greg. I live just up that lane at Macintosh's Farm." He spoke softly as he held his hand out toward me.

I couldn't believe that I just bumped into the man Sylvia described to me, not two hours ago. It was weird. Either I was thinking too much into all of these coincidences, or luck was on my side.

"I am Molly. Molly McGregor. It is nice to meet you. You're not going to believe this, but Sylvia was telling me about you this morning." The moment the words left my mouth, I felt the heat rise in my cheeks. Why I just said that, I don't bloody know.

"Really?" He asks, looking confused. "All good, I hope."

"If my offer gets accepted, I'll be looking for a local builder and joiner to help me convert Ethel's Farm."

"I must thank Sylvia, because she sends everyone my way."

"She really is lovely." I say, with a smile on my face.

"She is. If you need me to give you quotes and plans for work, just let me know when you move. I can run it passed your partner as well." That was it. I stood up shaking my head. A great start and then he had to spoil it with talking about partners.

"What is it with you country people?" I snap, attempting to walk away.

"Sorry, I don't follow," he replies, standing straight.

"You see a pregnant woman buying property and they must have partners, husbands, and the whole nine yards!"

"I'm sorry. I really didn't mean to offend you."

"Forget it." I start walking back to Sylvia's B&B. I just want to get out of here and out of Gregor's way before I say something else that I might regret.

I know my hormones are all over the place just now, but I am getting so sick of people just assuming that I am in a relationship.

"Molly. I really am sorry," said the masculine voice following behind me.

"It's fine. I'm sorry too."

"Hormones. I get it." I stop dead and turn to face him, waving my bottle of water in his face. "I didn't mean anything." He waves his hands out in front of him. "I am just going to shut up before you kill me." I smile and lower my bottle.

"Why are you following me?"

"No matter what you think of me, I am a gentleman. I'm not going to let you walk the mile back to Sylvia's in your condition, on your own."

"I'm pregnant, not ill," I snap, before I continue walking.

"Okay. Can we start again?" He places his hand on my arm making me look.

"Sure, but I don't need a babysitter."

"I know you don't. Although, Mia needs a walk and she likes you. We can walk you home if you'll let us. It sounds like I will be killing two birds with one stone."

"Playing the dog card, you must be desperate. Won't your *partner* wonder where you are?"

"What is it with you people assuming a man like me has a wife?" He snaps, making me look in his direction.

"I'm s-sorry," I stutter as he starts laughing. "Funny. Real funny." I shake my head and walk on slowly.

"I couldn't resist. We can now say we are even."

"If you say so." I want to laugh or show that I am totally over it all, but I keep my hard bitch routine up for a little while longer.

"I don't have a partner, wife, or anything else they get called. I do have a 5 year old daughter though. Her mother up and left when she was weeks old. She liked the good life too much and it didn't include a baby." I was surprised to hear that. I really don't understand people like her.

"I'm sorry to hear that. It seems your daughter's mother and my baby's father would get on like a house on fire."

"He isn't in the picture then?"

"No. He left when he found out about the baby. He told me to have an abortion, but the only thing that got aborted was him."

"Good for you! Do you have family here?"

"No. I just want a fresh start. New house. New baby. New business." After our rocky start, I was totally surprised at how well we were flowing together.

"What do you do?"

"I graduated with a degree in veterinary science. I've been running my own dog shelter in Aberdeen, but I want the barns and outhouses converted into an animal shelter."

"Well Molly, I admire your determination."

"It must be just as hard for you with work and your daughter." I try to give him some compliment for what he does every day. Not many men would step up to the mark and do what he does for his family.

"I have routines in place now and my mum and dad are great. They help us out," he said, enthusiastically.

"You run the farm and you get a free babysitter, sounds like a win-win situation."

"Something like that." He smiles back in my direction.

Our mile back to Sylvia's was quick. I guess the saying, *time passes quickly when you're having fun*, is very true.

"Thank you for walking me back, Greg. I really appreciate it. You didn't have to."

"I didn't have to, but I enjoyed it."

I keep my eye's looking straight forward, so he doesn't see me blush.

"Sylvia will think I've gotten lost." I tried to quickly change the subject back to neutral ground.

"She is a mother hen. You'll be in good hands with her around." It was funny that everyone thought of Sylvia the same way.

"I feel like I've known her my whole like," I explain.

"She has that effect on people."

"I actually have a lunch date with her this afternoon."

"Wow!" Greg exclaims.

"What?" I didn't know whether to take his response as a compliment or not.

"Sylvia does actually leave that B&B?" I wasn’t sure what he meant, so I wanted to know more.

"That is so shocking because..." I say nothing, waiting for Greg to continue.

"It isn't very often that you see Sylvia anywhere other than the B&B. You're a good influence on her."

"At least I influence someone." I wink in his direction, making him smile brightly again.

His smile is gorgeous. I don't know why I feel so warm and fuzzy when I speak to Greg, but I kind of like it.

"If you're still here at the weekend, would you like to rub some of that influence off on me?" I look quickly at him and laugh. "I don't mean it like *that*," stuttered Greg, showing his embarrassment.

I know he doesn't mean it to come out like that. If I thought for one moment that he was being a creep, he would have gotten a piece of my mind.

"Greg. Relax. What do you have in mind?"

"Maybe dinner?"

I became silent, as Greg stops in front of Sylvia's gates and turns to face me. "Of course, it would be purely business."

"Of course," I return.

"You could run all your plans by me and I could tell you if they would work."

His soft smile made me feel all giddy inside. I know he was only being nice to me. "Can I take your silence as a yes?"

"I don't know. I mean...I would like to." I pause and look down at my feet, but all I can see is my growing bump.

"But?"

I take a deep breath in and find my confidence.

"But...business or not, it isn't going to stop people from talking."

"Two young people discussing renovations. Not very much to gossip about if you ask me."

"What about a single father and a single pregnant lady wining and dining with fine cuisine?" It's almost as if, I'm trying to find my way out of this.

"If it would make you feel better, I can make dinner at my place."

"I am sure your parents would love that."

"I know they would, but I live in the cottage next to the farmhouse. We won't be putting anyone out. I can pull up all the plans for Ethel's Farm and we can discuss what you want done in peace and quiet. If you are really lucky, I can throw in a bottle or two of non-alcoholic wine." I can't believe how sweet and kind he sounds.

"Are you saying all of this hoping that I stick my ground and say no, or do you really want to spend your Saturday night talking work?" I raise a brow, not knowing what answer he will give me.

"First of all, I'm a farmer. Farmers work around the clock. So, spending the evening with a beautiful young lady who is glowing with child, discussing the business I love, with nice food and drink, sounds perfect to me."

Greg seems too good to be true. I didn't know he existed. Here I am, single, pregnant, and staring at the man I could never normally have. What harm can a business dinner do?

"Okay. If I'm still here on Saturday, I would love to join you. I don't have any farm plans."

"Don't worry about it. I have friends in the right places and I can get a copy for Saturday." His smile melts my heart.

"Thank you, Greg" I can see the sun sparkle in his eyes as my heart was pounding in my chest.

"There you are!" Greg and I both turn to see Sylvia practically jogging toward us. "I was getting worried about you wandering around on your own."

"Sorry, Sylvia. You can blame me," said Greg, confidently.

"Gregor Macintosh! Would you believe I was just talking about you this very morning?"

"Molly did tell me that my ears should have been burning." He glances at me, then back at Sylvia.

"It was all good, my son. I was putting more business your way."

"Sylvia here, is my number one fan," he said, resting his arm around Sylvia's shoulder carefully. I am happy to be standing here with these two people.

"Do you kids believe in fate?" Both Greg and I look at one another to see who is going to answer first. Sylvia has certainly put us on the spot with how forward she can be.

"Fate?" Greg responds, lingering off as he clearly thinks carefully about his answer. He gazes softly into my eyes, sending goosebumps through my entire body. "I believe that you should never force anything. Give everything your best shot, then let it be. If it's meant to be, it will be. If that is fate, then I guess I do believe in it after all. I just never realized it before."

Wow! It's one thing hoping and praying to find a sensitive man, but when one is standing in front of me, my knees are weak and my hormones are all over the place.

"Molly." Sylvia places her hand over my arm.

"Sorry. What?" I try to pull myself together. If I was trying to keep cool and calm, then I wasn't doing very well. Greg can clearly see why I am all over the place and that was one thing I didn't want to happen.

"Fate. Do you believe?"

"I believe things happen for a reason, but I don't think I qualify to answer like...Greg." I place my hand over my ever expanding tummy just to distract myself. I believed that my dating days were over. I have far more important things to worry myself with.

"It was lovely to meet you Molly. I'll see you about 7pm on Saturday, if you're still here." I was so glad that Greg could see how uneasy I was and managed to change the subject.

"Sure. I'll let you know," I was now trying to act cool.

"Here's my card. Give me a call either way." I watch him reach into his wallet, as Sylvia smiles softly in my direction. I know her mind is working overtime.

"Thank you." I accept his card and don't know what to say or do.

"Mia! Let's go girl." Greg whistles to his gorgeous dog. She's smelling about the flowers not paying any attention.

"Bye, Gregor. Don't you be a stranger, now," barks Sylvia, as Greg starts backing away waiting for Mia to join him.

"I won't, Sylvia. You know where I am if you need help with anything."

"Thanks, son. I'll remember that."

"Nice meeting you, Molly. I'm sorry. I've said that twice now."

"You too," I manage to say without bringing too much attention to myself. "I am just going to freshen up, Sylvia, then I'll be ready to go for lunch."

I start walking away from Sylvia before she can quiz me about my meeting with Greg.

"Okay doll. You take your time." Just walking down the driveway, I could still here Greg shouting and whistling to Mia. I laugh to myself, because he has his work cut out for him with his four legged friend.

I guess it's a good job he has the patience of a saint.

***

Sylvia pulls into a carpark of what I take to be the restaurant we are going to eat in for lunch. I look at the sign and read *The Web Spinner*. The building looks very traditional with a beautiful view of The Ochil Hills. It looks like a scene from a postcard.

Just the smell of the country air makes me feel very at home. Compared to the busy city life that I am used to, I could settle here. It is crazy to think we are in the City of Stirling, but we are so close to all of this beautiful country scenery. I love it all.

"What do you think, so far?" asks Sylvia as she locks up her car.

"It looks very beautiful. I bet lots of people just visit here to see the hills." The sight of the hills is drawing me in. I can't take my eyes away from them. I can imagine them in the winter covered with snow.

"Tourists from all over the world, come to visit the City of Stirling. I might live in the countryside, but we are only a couple of miles away from the city. Granted, it isn't Glasgow or Edinburgh, but it is beautiful in its own way. As far as I am aware, that is the only travel lodge in Stirling. It has been there for many years."

I turn slowly to look over at the lodge in the corner. The carpark looks very busy.

"Does this take a lot of business away from you?"

"I can't say it does. I have my regulars that keep coming back. If you haven't noticed already, I cater for the older, more mature residents. My regulars recommend me. Before I know what I am doing, it fills up nicely."

I follow Sylvia into the restaurant and we wait at the desk to be seated.

"Then I come up to your door. I'm surprised you didn't say there is no room at the inn," I say, as we both laugh.

"The minute I saw you standing in my reception hall, I knew instantly that we would get along. Then I see your bump." Sylvia places her hand over my belly. A warm, motherly feeling floats through me, leaving me all warm and protected. "I knew with the look on your face that you had the weight of the world on your shoulders. You reminded me of myself at your age."

"You could tell all of that from one look?" I ask.

"Life experience, dolly. You don't get to be my age without seeing and hearing it all."

"Is it a table for two, ladies?" asks the waiter, as he approaches us.

"Yes, please," said Sylvia. "Do you have any tables overlooking the hills? My friend is visiting and I would love to show her all the great things Stirling has to offer."

"Of course. It's your lucky day, because we are very slow." We follow our waiter to the back of the restaurant. I can't believe the view. The big bay window opened up and the view was stunning. If I didn't want to live here before, then I certainly do now.

"Can I get you ladies a drink?"

"Can I have a black coffee, please?" asks Sylvia.

"I'll have a fresh orange juice and lemonade, please," I say, as well-mannered as I can be.

"Sure. Coming right up." I was amazed with my view of The Ochil Hills staring back at me.

"Beautiful. Isn't it?" Sylvia broke the silence.

"It is! Do you ever get bored of looking at the same scenery?" I realize that this might sound like a silly question, but I needed to know that what I was feeling wasn't going to fade in a few months.

"Not for me, but I guess for a young person, it could become tiresome."

"Would you ever leave?" I thought I knew the answer already.

"If a millionaire swept me off my feet to some exotic country, then yes. That's not going to happen, so I'll be here until the day I take my last breath."

"I hope that when I look back in twenty years, I can be happy and content just like you are now."

"I know you will be, Molly. I think we get on so well, because you remind me of myself in so many ways." She stopped talking to take a sip of her coffee.

I place my chin on top of my hands I can see in her eyes that she's haunted by something. I can't believe that she has hid it so well.

"Looking at you now, I see myself, because I was exactly like you. Young, single, ambitious, pregnant..." Sylvia trailed off and now I was confused, because she had never mentioned having kids before.

"I sense these aren't good memories for you, so don't feel like you need to tell me."

"I never share this with anyone, but I feel like I can tell you now. I feel like it is my time to get it off my chest."

I could see how confident Sylvia was and I wasn't going to stop her from talking if she really wanted to confide in me.

"Your story brought it all home to me. I was in love with Malcolm Farrow, or I thought I was. We shared everything with one another until I found out I was pregnant with his child. He left me high and dry."

"I didn't know that you had a family, Sylvia"

"I don't," she said, calmly.

I was confused to say the least, but I felt like I needed to know everything about Sylvia. "Back when I was pregnant, there were no scans or tests. I thought when I decided to keep the baby, that was it. I would live my life bringing up my own flesh and blood. Malcolm gave me an ultimatum, him or the baby."

"You chose the same thing I did." I smile softly and grip Sylvia's hand over the table. "I don't think I know a woman, that wouldn't choose their baby first."

"I didn't get the happily ever after. I had an ectopic pregnancy and I lost the baby. I nearly lost my life in the process, but it made me realize that life was for living."

"Sylvia. I am so sorry. It must be hard for you to watch me parade around pregnant." I felt like a knife had been stuck in my chest listening to Sylvia tell me about her life.

"Don't be silly, Molly. I love seeing you glow. I love seeing how happy you are to carry your bundle of joy. I've had many years to come to terms with what happened to me. Malcolm and my miscarriage gave me the life I've got today."

"Did you never want any other children?"

"Of course I did, but the damage caused by the ectopic pregnancy made me unable to have any children. I was devastated at the time, but I've got many nieces and nephews. I got the best of both worlds. I get to baby sit and give presents, but I have to hand them back when all is said and done."

She was brave and confident. I was fighting back the tears about her loss, but of course that could be my hormones playing with my emotions.

"I didn't tell you, to upset you," said Sylvia, squeezing my hand with both of hers. "I told you, because I know that you've made the right decision. You will have a very happy life here."

"I wish I had your confidence, Sylvia." I was never a confident person growing up. I always doubted myself. Now that I am alone and pregnant, I am always doubting my ability to be a good mother.

"You do! You just don't see it yet. Confidence takes years to gain. I haven't always been like this. It took me years after I lost the baby to see what life was all about."

"What if I screw up? I have a little life depending on me."

"If you want me to sit here and say you won’t ever screw anything up, then you will have a long wait. Parenthood doesn't come with a manual. We all make mistakes but we learn from them. As long as you have love to give, that’s all you need. No man is ever going to love and provide anything that you can't. You don't need a man to bring up your child or run your business, so stop worrying. I'll be here to help you with the childcare, if and when you need it. Everything will fall into place if you really want it to."

I wipe away a stray tear, as I hear my phone ringing in my bag. Like a mad woman, I scramble around in my bag to get it before I miss the call.

"Oh no! It's my solicitor!" I felt my body freeze.

"What are you waiting for? Answer it, quickly!" Sylvia shrieks. I was shaking terribly as I pushed *answer*.

"Hello. Molly speaking. How can I help you?"

"Hey, Molly. It's Jacob Jones."

"Oh, hi, Jacob. I take it you have some news for me?" I tried to keep calm, even though I was going out of my mind.

I look over at Sylvia and she has her fingers crossed on both hands held up to her mouth.

"I do. Yes. I'm not going to drag it out for you. Your offer has been accepted."

"Really?" I was in complete shock.

"Of course they accepted. They would have been crazy not to. Did you really expect me to come back with bad news?" For some reason, I didn't expect to get given Ethel's Farm without a fight.

"Honestly Jacob, I had no idea what to expect. I didn't want to get my hopes up."

"I knew with your offer, that it was a done deal."

"So what happens now?" I was going crazy inside wondering what I was going to do.

"I am waiting to receive all the documents you need to sign. Mr. Leroy, the estate agent has them and he is going to get his end tied up today. I'm going to pick them up at 11am tomorrow."

"Wait a minute! You're coming here tomorrow?"

"Of course I am. You're there and it makes sense for us to get all the paperwork done in the one place. I'll stop by tomorrow, around lunchtime. I've googled the B&B you are staying in and I have the postcode, so I should find it fairly easily." I thought I was dreaming.

"Great! I'll see you tomorrow." I was overwhelmed.

"Don't sound so shocked, Molly."

"I am on the verge of being speechless and we both know that doesn't happen very often."

"Some people would pay good money to see you speechless." He said, sarcastically.

"Cheeky." I laughed, nervously.

"Oh, before I forget, does your B&B have any spare rooms for tomorrow night?"

"I'm not sure, Jacob. Hold on, because I have Sylvia here. I'll ask her for you." I covered my phone and asked, "Sylvia. Do you have a room available tomorrow night?"

"Only a single, if that's any good."

"One single room," I explained to Jacob.

"I'll take it, if that's okay. It will save me booking elsewhere."

"Can my solicitor take your single room?" I felt like I was the go-between between Jacob and Sylvia, when I should have just put him on speakerphone and he could have done the talking himself.

"Of course he can."

"Your room's booked." I told him.

"Thank you, Molly. I'll see you soon."

"Bye," I said quickly, putting the phone down.

If I didn't feel like celebrating before, I do now. I want to shout my news from the rooftop.

"Well?" Asked Sylvia, still crossing her fingers in front of her mouth.

"You are now looking at the new owner of Ethel's Farm!" I screeched rather loudly, while clapping my hands.

"That's fantastic!" d Sylvia stood up to pull me into her embrace. "This calls for a celebration. Lunch is on me. The Champagne will go on ice until this little one is born."

"I can't believe it, Sylvia!" I felt exasperated from one phone call. What was I going to be like watching my dreams come to life over the next few months?

Both Sylvia and I sat back down in our seats. Customers nearby must have been thinking that we were crazy, jumping about like looneys.

I just couldn't believe that this was my lucky day I couldn't wait to phone everyone and post my news on Facebook and Twitter.

Every one of my family and friends had faith in me. I was the only one who doubted it. I told myself if the farm fell through, that there was plenty more fish in the sea. I would have just had to wait until someplace else came open.

However, here I was celebrating the start of my new life. My fresh start in the country. *A Country Escape.*

"Well, Molly. It looks like you will be having that date with Gregor, after all," said Sylvia, with a big ass grin on her face.

"Oh, behave yourself. When did business turn into a date?" I teased her back unable to stop smiling. I had a funny feeling that this smile was going to be stuck on my face for a very long time.

"Young Gregor will do a fantastic job on your farm. I would recommend him to the Queen."

"That good, huh?"

"The best."

I know that Sylvia was hoping that Greg and I would become romantically involved, but I can't think about that any time soon. I have a house to refurbish from top to bottom, a barn conversion to do, and a business to launch, all in the space of a short few months before the baby arrives.

Yeah, I have a funny feeling that the next few months are going to be crazy.

***

The last 24 hours were absolutely crazy. I thought I was never going to sleep last night. After my lunch date with Sylvia, we came back home and I sat in the lounge until 10pm going through designs I wanted for the house and my ideas for the business. Most importantly, I ordered the baby's nursery furniture. Sylvia came to my rescue and told me to get the baby's things delivered here, because she can put them in her summer house until I need them.

I still can't believe how lucky I am to find a friend like Sylvia, because there aren't many like her anymore.

By the time I hit the pillow, I literally slept like a baby. I woke up this morning bright and breezy. I had to pinch myself, because I thought yesterday had been one long dream. I was relieved to realize that yesterday did happen.

Once I sign the paperwork today, it's the start of my future.

"Hey, Greg. Thank you for dropping by." I heard Sylvia talking out in the front reception area. I knew Greg was *the* Greg I didn't want to see just yet.

"It's no problem at all, Sylvia. You know I will do anything for you, if I can."

"I appreciate that, son. Come through and I'll get you a coffee." That was what I didn't want to hear.

"I'll have a tea, if that's okay." responded Greg, softly.

"You can have anything you like, sweetheart. Take a seat." I looked up from my laptop and mountains of notes, as Greg noticed me.

"Hi, Molly," said Greg, as he approached my table.

"Hi Greg. It's nice to see you again." I didn't know how to act around Greg.

"Can I join you for five minutes?" I stupidly looked him in the eyes and I felt my face blush a thousand shades of red.

"Sure," I replied, while I cleared my notebooks into a neat pile at my side of the table.

"How are you both?" I looked to him curiously raising my eyebrows wondering what he was talking about. "You and the baby?"

"Oh..." I felt stupid now, not realizing what he meant. "We're fine. Thank you for asking."

I think I was just gobsmacked that a man was asking how my unborn child and me was. Usually a man would see a single, pregnant woman and run for the hills.

"How are you?" I asked quickly, realizing it would be rude not to ask him the same question.

"I'm good. Sylvia asked me to stop by to fix a leaking tap, so here I am." he smiled at me with his cute button smile.

"You're a gentleman to your neighbors."

"I wouldn't see anyone stuck," he said.

I picked up my cup of tea, which was cold now and took a drink just to distract myself.

"Did you put an offer in for Ethel's Farm?" I suddenly realized that Greg didn't know any of my good news and I felt excited all over again.

"Yeah. My offer was accepted yesterday. You're now looking at your new neighbor."

"Congratulations!" he said, enthusiastically.

"Thanks."

"So, will I see you on Saturday for dinner?"

"I don't want to put you out. Maybe we should schedule it for during the week when your daughter is at school and you aren't so busy."

"Saturday is perfect, Molly. I appreciate you thinking about my daughter, but she will be in bed. It's the perfect time for me. If I am being totally honest, you will be giving me something to do. Since having a child, my weekends have become a little boring. I would much rather be working with good company."

I suddenly realized that I had a lot of boring nights to look forward to, so I felt like I should be on the same page as Greg.

"Only if you're sure."

"I wouldn't have offered if I wasn't sure."

"I just thought since you like to help a damsel in distress, you just couldn't say no." I liked to hear the soft laughter that escaped him.

"I could never say no to you, Molly. You'll be doing me a favor."

"Okay. I look forward to it."

"Sorry I took so long, Greg. Here is your tea." Sylvia arrived in the nick of time.

"Thanks, Sylvia."

"You're welcome. It's the least I can do since you dropped everything to help me." Sylvia knew exactly what she was doing and I wouldn't be surprised if she broke the tap herself, just to get me and Greg in the same room.

"It really is no trouble at all."

"Did Molly tell you about her good news?" I rolled my eyes in Sylvia's direction and waited until she was finished.

"Yeah, we were just discussing it," he responded with a knowing smile.

"Fabulous! Ain't it? It's about time we get some young talent about here."

"Aye. Ethel's Farm could use a new, young, talented, fresh face," said Greg, never taking his eyes away from me.

I was a little surprised that he could label me all those lovely things. He truly was a gentleman, even though he didn't know me.

"So, this leaking tap of yours...?"

"Aye. I was in cleaning and freshening up the back room for Molly's solicitor and the sink in the bathroom wouldn't go off. Do you think you can sort it for me? Just give me the bill for your time and parts." She smiled as she glanced at me, then Greg.

"Don't be silly, Sylvia. A tap can be fixed in no time. You did me a favor today, because I could have killed Sam this morning."

"See Molly? This young man is a diamond. Minus the killing his brother bit." I smiled and nodded, but I didn't want to open my mouth in case I said the wrong thing. I knew Greg was one in million, but Sylvia didn't need any encouragement at pushing us closer together. "Finish your tea and I'll show you where to go. Take your time."

Sylvia couldn't be any more obvious if she tried. Both Greg and I couldn't contain our laughter, as Sylvia moved out into the reception area.

"Has our Sylvia not driven you away back to Aberdeen yet?" teased Greg.

"She is hard work, but I really do love her to pieces. I can't wait to finally move." I was desperate to get into my own house and get settled. If I had a magic wand, I would have used it by now.

"How long will you have to wait until you can move?"

"I'm really not sure. The farm is ready and my funds are waiting to be transferred. I just hope once the paperwork is done today, it won't take very long."

"I hope you don't think I'm trying to take over, but I know you will probably need to be settled with the baby coming along. When you see your solicitor today, ask him to put in the forms for gaining planning permission to convert the barn." I watched Greg reach into his pocket and take out a brown envelope. "These are my company's details and a rough draft of what needs to be done before we can start. Usually this is all they need for private property. I took a quick look at the barn. Of course, you don't need to use it. I just thought it would save time for you and get the ball rolling."

I was speechless. Again. I knew Greg was thoughtful and kind, but to go out of his way to do this for me, he was an angel.

"I don't know what to say, Greg. I really appreciate you doing this."

"Of course. You can call this a favor from a friend." I looked at the envelope and back at him with a huge smile on my face.

"Thank you! Please give me a bill for this and I'll get it taken care of immediately."

"Not at all. There is no charge for this," He said, sincerely.

"Sylvia was right. You are a diamond." I couldn't believe I just said that, but it was the truth.

"Two compliments in one day? I better be careful, because my head might not fit through the door."

I felt like a teenager, because I couldn't stop myself from giggling at Greg. Even the baby kicked me hard because of my fit of laughter.

"For Saturday, is there anything you don't like or can't eat? I don't want to cook something you can't eat. When my ex was pregnant with our daughter, she didn't care about the baby long enough to look into what she could or couldn't eat, so I guess you could say I'm new to all of this."

"You are very kind, Greg, but honestly I don't want you going out of your way. I am staying away from anything with raw eggs and coffee, but I'm sure I will love whatever you cook."

"Great! I'll see you on Saturday. If you see anything online or in magazines that you want incorporated into your house or barn conversion, let me know about it. It's good for me to get a feel for your style and preference."

"Really?" I asked.

"Yeah. I could go in guns blazing and put my touch on the place, but it's yours. It needs to be what you like."

"Okay. I don't know why I never thought of that." Baby brain was truly taking over my logical thinking.

"Well, it was nice talking to you Molly, but I better get this tap fixed. My brother needs me this afternoon."

"Do you ever get a minute to yourself?" I asked, before he walked away.

"After 5 'o' clock. I like to be in the house with my daughter for dinner. We get to do homework together and then spend a couple of hours together before bed."

I didn't think anything would shock me but the more I heard about Greg, the more jealous I become.

"Your daughter is a very lucky little girl to have a dad like you."

"I'm sure she might not agree at times, but thank you for yet another compliment."

"Go! Before I have to stick pins in your head. You won't fit out that door if you get any more compliments." We both laughed before he stood and left me sitting alone in the lounge.

After he left, I felt really alone. I felt like a piece of me left with him. I didn't understand how one person could make me feel so good about myself.

I longed for a man I couldn't have. For all of my adult life, I dreamed of having a man like Greg, but I came to the conclusion that he didn't exist. I gave up on Mr. Right. Even now that I know one does exist, the most that is going to happen is friendship. I have the baby and he has his daughter. We each have someone depending on us.

Friendship is all we need. I guess.

***

Greg

I managed to tear myself away from Molly and the lounge area to fix Sylvia's tap. I leaned over Sylvia's reception area desk and took a few deep breaths before I did something stupid.

Molly was like a breath of fresh air. Since I had my daughter, I haven’t felt this way about a woman. I just can't seem to get her out of my mind. I wake up thinking about her and I go to sleep thinking about her.

I know I have to fight my feelings, because we both have someone to take care of. We are both adults and I will survive having her as a friend.

It is better than nothing.

"Sorry, Greg. Are you waiting on me showing you where to go?" I heard Sylvia's voice from behind me. I straightened up and pulled myself together.

"Yeah. You can lead the way." I smiled in Sylvia's direction. I could see with the big silly grin on her face, that she knew exactly what was wrong with me.

"I can see me having to bang your two heads together," said Sylvia, walking in front of me.

"Huh?" I tried to keep a straight face but when Sylvia turned around and just looked at me, I felt my knees go weak and the butterflies in my stomach took over.

"You might try to fool yourself son, but you can't fool an old fool like me. I can see the way you look at Molly. Believe me when I say this, she looks at you the same way. You're both too stubborn to see it."

We reached the bedroom where we were supposed to be and I leaned against the bathroom doorframe, as Sylvia turned to look at me.

"Sylvia. I'm not going to push Molly into anything. She has obviously been through just as much as I have. I would rather have her friendship, than to ruin it between us and having nothing."

"She'll see that you're good for her. She's blind right now, because she needs to do what she thinks is right for the baby. Have patience with her."

I bit my lip until I felt the sting snap me back to the here and now. I would have been happier thinking it was all in my head. I didn't want to know that Sylvia thought Molly was thinking like I was.

This has just put a spanner in the works. On Saturday, I will have to put it all out of my head and act like the gentleman that Molly thinks I am.

Molly

"Molly! It's lovely to see you," said Jacob, as he took me into his arms and placed a peck on my cheek. "I am sorry I'm late. There was a big accident on the motorway, then I had to wait for Mr. Leroy to finish with a client. Anyway, I am here now and the paperwork is ready for me to go through with you. Then hopefully we can get it signed and go from there."

"Great. Come through to the lounge and we can get a cup of tea." My nerves were in full swing. I had no idea why.

"I'm choking for a coffee. Mr. Leroy's receptionist gave me a coffee and I am sure it was that cheap rubbish." I had to laugh at Jacob's tone. Even I know that he likes a good cup of coffee.

"Take a seat, Jacob. Sylvia's coffee is to die for. I smell it every morning when I get up." I have been off coffee for a few months and it hasn't bothered me until I started staying with Sylvia. The smell every morning wakes up my cravings.

"You take a seat as well Molly and I will bring your drinks," said Sylvia, stalking around the kitchen door.

"Thank you, Sylvia." If I didn't know better, I would say that Sylvia had some weird sense of hearing, because she was always on par with everything going on.

I sat down and watched Jacob lay all the paper work out on the table. I felt like a giddy teenager for the second time today.

"Has it all sunk in yet? You sounded quite shell shocked on the phone yesterday." Jacob sat back in his seat, studying me carefully.

Thinking back to the phone call yesterday, shell-shocked was a bit of an understatement. I felt like I was floating on a cloud. "I guess it has."

"You don't seem too happy for someone who really wants this."

"I really am happy, Jacob."

"But...?" I really hated how Jacob knew me so well. Even before he was my solicitor, he was dealing with my family's business. His family before him, was dealing with my grandfather's business, so we are very familiar with each other.

"I'm just so used to bad luck, that I expected someone to come along and drag it all away from me." I felt tears threaten to make an appearance, but I didn't want to fall apart.

"Molly." Jacob's hand stretched over the table and took my hand in his. "You can't keep looking to the past. You've got to look into the future, no matter how hard it is going to be. No one is taking anything from you. Especially not on my watch. Your luck has changed for the better and you need to start believing in yourself. When I heard what Bradley did to you, I could have punched some sense into him."

"You've worked for my dad for too long. You sound just like him." I joked trying to lighten the moment.

"That might not be a bad thing. Remember when I took over from my father and your dad was his top client? He trusted me with his business and affairs. I don't think I would be where I am today, if it wasn't for your father."

"He is a strong willed person," I stated, without getting my dad embedded into my head further.

"The apple doesn't fall far from the tree, Molly. You're more like your father than you think."

"Everyone tells me that. I guess I should start believing in myself."

"Here we go, kids!" I laughed at Sylvia, as she placed a tray down on the table beside Jacob and me. "Mr. Solicitor. You have been here five minutes and you've upset my girl. Don't do that again."

"I'm fine, Sylvia. I just got a bit emotional. That's all." I didn't think I could get any closer to Sylvia, but then she comes out with a comment like that and she leaves me speechless.

"Turn that frown upside down and put a smile on that face of yours. I don't like to see you upset." I loved how Sylvia could say one thing to me and then just take everything bad away.

"I’m fine. I've got it out of my system now." I tried to sound confident but I knew that she would see through my act.

"Good. I'll leave you both to it." I watched Sylvia, as she left the lounge with me and Jacob sitting so still and quiet. We could hear a pin drop.

"You've got a good friend there, Molly."

"I know. Sylvia is great." I picked up the milk and started to pour it into my tea. I needed a distraction and this was the only thing I could think of. I needed to get all of this paperwork out of the way, so that I could move onto the next part of my new adventure.

My emotions were all over the place, but I knew that I would get there in the end.

CHAPTER 4

Where It All Begins

Molly

Saturday was fast approaching and I was no further forward. I thought when my solicitor finished all the paperwork, I would be ready to jump in with both feet. Now I need to wait for planning permission. I need to wait for my keys. I need to keep everything on hold and I have no patience. I want it all done yesterday.

I thought they might see a pregnant lady in need of getting everything done. Oh no! They just see a lady and think they can take the piss out of me. Jacob has been very good keeping everyone on their toes, but nothing is happening quickly enough for me. I can see a nervous breakdown in my immediate future.

I was fed up checking emails and looking at designs, so I decided to get ready for my dinner with Greg. I know I shouldn't be pleased about spending the evening with him, but I needed to get out of this B&B. I love Sylvia dearly, but I need the company of someone close to my own age.

I have done everything Greg asked of me. Planning permission forms were submitted. I may I have gone a little over the top with magazines and designs. I might drive him crazy tonight asking questions and throwing everything at him.

It's annoyed me all week about what I was going to wear tonight. Then it dawned on me that I think of Greg as a friend, so I can just be relaxed and casual. I certainly wasn't going to get myself all worked up.

I slipped my jacket on and grabbed my bag. It was now or never. If I didn't leave the B&B while I felt confident, I would make up several excuses not to go.

I spotted Sylvia sitting at her desk in the reception area, but she was too far away to hear me. I just didn't want to frighten the life out of her by sneaking up behind her.

"I don't know what time I will be home, Sylvia," I said, as I approached her slowly. "Will I just come in the side door?"

"Aye, Molly. I'll leave it open for you, my love. I hope Gregor is a good host."

"I'm sure he will be. After all, tonight is a business meeting and he appears to be good at what he does."

"You keep telling yourself that, my love." Sylvia really was impossible. I wanted to stamp it on her forehead that Greg and I were just friends. Nothing else.

I had a funny feeling that I was wasting my time, so I just started heading towards the door. "Have fun."

"You too." I was never so glad to get outside and take a deep breath of fresh air. It's amazing how much confidence you get from a lung full of fresh air.

I made my way to my car and was lost in my thoughts, along the road to Greg's house. I knew where the cut-off to his farm was, but I hoped that I knocked on the right door. He told me that his cottage was the one in the back.

I'm just not sure that I am ready to meet his parents yet. I want to have a chilled out night, but after Sylvia and her match making ideas, I feel exhausted.

I turn into the lane where Greg's farm is and I can see the farm starting to get closer. The ground was similar to Ethel's farm, just better kept. I pulled up in front of the big house and got out to grab my bags. I was hoping that it was easy enough to walk from here.

"Can I help you, hen?" came a soft voice from behind me, as I lifted my bags from the boot of my car.

"I'm looking for Gregor. We have a business meeting tonight."

"Oh, you must be Molly. I believe we are going to be neighbors." All I could do was smile at the middle aged lady in front of me, because her presence made me feel calm and welcome.

"Yes, I am Molly. It's nice to meet you." I extended my hand out to the lady, now standing a few feet away from me.

"I'm Greg's mum. My name is Caroline. Follow me." I should have realized that this was Greg's mum when she said we were going to be neighbors.

"Thank you." I suddenly felt shy, as I followed Caroline. I had no idea why, because she appeared to be a lovely lady.

"You will know where to go the next time you come." I got a funny feeling that Caroline was another Sylvia.

"Yeah. I wasn't sure if it was okay to park here," I said, nervously.

"Of course it is. Treat it like your own when you're here." I couldn't help but think Carline expected me to drop by a lot. Maybe she wasn't being as bold as Sylvia was, but I could still sense her eagerness. I did have to smile, because I know Sylvia cares about me, just like Caroline cares about her son. "Here we are. This is Greg's cottage."

"Thank you, Caroline. It was lovely to meet you."

"You to, my lovely." Before I could even walk up the couple of steps to get to Greg's front door, Caroline was walking back into the direction of her own house.

It really is lovely down here. Seeing this farm fully operational, it let me see what Ethel's farm could be like in a few months.

I knocked softly on the door and waited. I suddenly got nervous and I could have kicked myself.

"Hey, Molly!" Greg reached down and placed a soft kiss on my cheek. I was taken a back, but I realized he was just being friendly.

"Hi. Your mum just showed me here."

"I'm glad you found it okay. Come in." I followed Greg into his house. It was a typical farmer's cottage, but it was so comfortable. I could tell that an architect lives here, it had the odd touch here and there that only a designer would have.

"Can I take your jacket?"

"Thanks." I put my bags down and took my jacket off.

"Daddy?" I looked around at a little girl walking through the doorway. "Sorry. Can I get a drink before bed?"

"Of course you can, Kayleigh. Help yourself. Before you go, I would like you to meet Molly. I'm going to be helping Molly with her new home."

"Boring."

"Kayleigh!" scolded Greg.

"Sorry. Hi Molly."

"Hi Kayleigh. It's lovely to meet you. Your dad has told me so much about you."

"Are you having a baby?" I felt my cheeks flush a little as I noticed my hand was resting on my tummy.

"Yes. Yes, I am."

"That's cool. I would like a baby brother or sister, but my dad said that's never going to happen." I laughed softly at the little girl, as I saw Greg shake his head with a big grin on his face.

" I would have said that a long time ago, but now look at me," I replied, with a smile.

"Will you still be working with my dad, when the baby's born?" I looked up at Greg for his help, because I didn't want to say the wrong thing.

"Molly is moving into Ethel's Farm, just along the road. I'm sure you will be seeing the baby, Kayleigh."

"Cool. Good night, daddy. Good night Molly."

"Goodnight, sweetie," I said, smiling softly as she gave her dad a cuddle before going to bed. I couldn't believe how sweet Greg was with her. He reminded me of my dad when I was that age.

"I'm sorry about that, Molly. She's usually in bed by now, but she knew I had someone coming over."

"Don't worry about it. I would love to get to know her. She seems like a wonderful little girl."

"She's my life, but she loves asking questions."

"I can imagine. I think they all go through that faze." I smiled, as I followed Greg into the dining room.

"Take a seat and I'll get us a drink."

"Thank you." I took a seat at the dining table and I felt myself relax. I had no idea where my nerves came from before, because I knew that Greg would make me feel comfortable. He has a calming aura about him.

"I knew you wouldn't like anything alcoholic, so I picked up a bottle of non-alcoholic wine while I was out."

"You really didn't have to go to the bother, Greg. Tea or water would have been great."

"It was no trouble." I watched him, as he filled our glasses up and placed the bottle into the wine cooler in the center of the table. Everything was perfect. He has really gone to the effort of making everything lovely.

I just want him to do something to slip up. I want something to stop me from wanting what I can't have.

"How is everything going with the farm?"

"It isn't," I said, sulking.

"Why? What happened?" He sat beside me at the head of the table.

"It isn't going quick enough for me. The planning permission forms have been put in. Now they say it could take twelve weeks. I get my keys on the 23rd, so I'll have to work on the house first. It makes sense, but I wanted it all done together." Greg sat there like a gentleman taking it all in.

"Well, to give you a bit of hope, I just finished a conversion in Stirling and they got the planning permission within two weeks. I know you want in and to be settled before the baby comes along. I'll run my men ragged to get it done."

"Don't be silly. I can't ask you to kill your men."

"You didn't. I'm a slave driver when it comes to my business. I have a couple of my men here on the farm working and they tell everyone that I'm like two different bosses. Here on the farm, I'm easy going with a laugh and a joke. However, when I'm doing the architect, I go into a world of my own. I like it done to the highest standards. If that means they work around the clock, then so be it."

"I think I would like to see the bossy side of you. I can't imagine you being anything of the sort." I teased.

"I don't do as much with my own business now. I let the team get on with it, unless there are big projects."

"It will be your team doing my place?" I asked.

"No. I feel like *I* need to do Ethel's Farm. I grew up here and I used to go to Ethel's Farm when I was Kayleigh's age. I don't think my team could do it justice without me."

"You really do take your work seriously."

"I do, but come 5 'o' clock every night, I come home to Kayleigh."

"It's nice to know that there are men that are committed to their family." After the words tumbled from my tongue, I wanted to kick myself for being so bloody honest.

"I can't imagine my life without Kayleigh. Some people see me as a single parent and feel sorry for me, but it isn't that bad. Once you get over the sleepless and lonely nights, it's a doddle."

"You're not making it sound very good. Shouldn't you be putting my mind at ease?"

"You will be a great mum, Molly." I couldn't stop myself from letting out a little snigger at Greg's response. "You will."

"You know that from our few meetings? Two of which weren't planned."

"I knew it the moment I saw you. Tonight, when you spoke to Kayleigh, it was confirmed for me." I was curious now.

"I don't make a habit of bringing work home, but I've had a couple of meetings where Kayleigh has been around and no one interacts with her."

"Ignorant buggers!" I said again without thinking.

"Exactly! Only a parent would understand how angry it makes me, when they can't even say hello or goodbye."

"To put your mind at ease, I don't mind spending time with your daughter. In fact, she's welcome at Ethel's Farm any time."

"Thank you."

"You're welcome." I took a sip of my drink just so I could break eye contact with Greg. I could feel the heat rise in my cheeks.

"I'll go and plate up dinner and we can talk about your plans. I hope you like roast beef. My mum said it was one meat that anyone loves."

"You should listen to your mum, because it is one of my favorites."

Greg stood slowly with that schoolboy smile plastered on his face. Either he was shocked at how well our meeting was going, or he was shocked that I agreed with his mum.

For what it was worth, I'm glad I came.

***

It was hard to believe how well tonight has gone. Waiting for Greg to bring us tea to finish off our night, was blissful. His cottage was so relaxed. The chat flowed nicely. I was now looking forward to working with him on my house and business.

"I hope I've managed to answer all of your questions tonight," he said, as he came back from his kitchen carrying a tray.

"You've done more than answer my questions. I was starting to doubt this was even possible until I came here tonight."

"This is all possible, Molly. You just need to trust the professionals. I wouldn't dream of questioning your ability of looking after Mia, if she was ill, so try to think of me the same way. I will give you the house of your dreams."

"I never doubted you, Greg. I think I've just been overwhelmed this week, being so far away from family and friends. It made me think twice."

" I don't know you as well as your friends back home, but I hope that we can become good friends." Our eyes locked and goosebumps appeared on my arms. I had to break eye contact before one of us did or said something we would regret.

"Me too. I would really like that."

"You can't go without tasting my mum's shortbread. She sent some over today when she knew I was having a meeting tonight."

"I don't usually have a sweet tooth, but since I became pregnant, I would have fun in a Sweetie Factory." I am never keen at sharing my life with anyone, but tonight my thoughts and feelings just flowed. I wasn't afraid to talk to Greg and that felt nice.

"You *are* eating for two."

"Don't you start. I hear that every day from Sylvia."

"Are you staying at Sylvia's when your house is getting done?" I stopped lifting my cup rather quickly, because I hadn't even thought about that. I have been too busy thinking about conversions and baby stuff. My living arrangements never entered my mind. "I take it by your silence, that you haven't thought that far ahead."

"No. I'll see what it's like when I get in. It is livable. It would be easier if I could stay at my own house. I just don't want to get in your way, or cause any harm to the baby."

I felt rather silly now. I thought I had everything under control.

"You will at least have somewhere comfortable to sleep."

"The main things are taken care of, Greg. I trust you with the barn. I've told you what I want and where. The rest is up to you. I'm not afraid of lifting a paint brush, so I can help in the house."

"I don't think so, Molly. I can't accept you falling or hurting yourself or the baby. Leave all the heavy work to the painters and decorators. That's why you hired them, after all."

"I just don't like to be doing nothing."

"Think of it as maternity leave. You're resting until the little one makes an appearance."

"For a man, you sure do give good advice." I smiled, realizing that he was the one blushing now.

"A couple of weeks working together and you will be trying to get me to shut up."

I shifted in my seat just so I could pick my cup of tea back up. I didn't want to tell him that I was enjoying his company. I didn't want to ruin our friendship before it even began. It's better to have Greg as a friend than not having him in my life at all.

"It's been a lovely evening. I really should be getting back to the B&B. Sylvia is leaving the side door open for me and I don't want it open all night."

"Are my tea making skills that bad?"

"No. Not at all, Greg. It's great. I just realized that it's 11pm. Don't farmers get up at the crack of dawn?" It occurred to me just how little I knew about farmers.

"Only during certain seasons. Spring is a busy time, because all the animals are giving birth. We have the fields to get prepared for planting. That's when 12 hour days can turn into 16-18 hour days. Summer can be just as busy, but I tend to leave my brother alone then. He takes care of shearing the sheep. The winter wheat is harvested and the straw is dried and bundled for bedding. Come autumn, most grains and other spring planted crops are harvested. After the summer growing season and the autumn harvest, we aren't as busy in the fields, but there is still plenty of work to be done. Cows and other milking animals, still need to be milked every day."

There was a sparkle in his eye, as he continued.

"The animals depend on us more in the winter months for their food. They may need to eat more to stay warm. By December, we've moved our animals indoors to protect them from the cold weather. It means there's more cleaning to be done indoors to keep old food, bedding, and manure from building up. We think about the past year and make plans for the next season. This time of year, we make all the repairs to the farm equipment, buildings, and tools. These need to be ready in time for spring and for the new growing season."

I was gobsmacked listening to Greg discuss the farm. I never thought I would be interested in this kind of stuff, but I really am.

"For an architect that loved in the city, you sure know what you're talking about when it comes to the farm."

"When my dad took ill and he couldn't do as much on his own, I hated the thought of coming back home. However, I hated the idea of him losing his pride and joy. I said I would give it 6 months, but that 6 months has turned into nearly 5 years."

"You enjoy it. Don't you, Greg?"

"I hated it when I couldn't do what I loved. Then I came up with the idea of running my own business from here as well. Now I juggle the two. I can do my building and drawing in the quieter months."

"I know where to come when I want a lesson on farm life. I've always wondered what goes on with the day to day running of a farm."

"Well now you know."

"I do. I also know that you will be needing your beauty sleep for tomorrow, so I will leave you to rest."

"You don't have to rush off," he said, being insistent.

"I know, but I've taken up more than enough of your time. I look forward to seeing your drawings. I'll be in touch. It will be all go from the 23rd when I get my keys, so I intend to take things easy."

"Sounds like a plan." I stood up slowly, now realizing how big my bump was getting. It was getting in the way more often and I felt huge. I walked out into the reception hall where I knew my jacket was. It felt like I had been here longer than a few hours. Time flies by when you're having fun.

"Don't be a stranger, Molly. Call me if you have any questions." I let Greg help me put my jacket on. I felt like a princess getting his help. Not many men would take the time to help me.

Just feeling his hands brush against my skin had me tingling. I hated hormones. I needed to try to control myself before I embarrassed the two of us.

"I'll walk you out to your car."

"Will Kayleigh be okay?"

"Yeah. Once she's asleep nothing wakes her. A bomb could go off and she would be none the wiser." I had to laugh, because I can remember loving my sleep. My parents had to drag me out of bed on many occasions, much to my annoyance. "Let me take those bags for you. I don't think you left any magazines in the shop."

"This is only some of them."

"Your ideas are great without the magazines. This is where it all begins, Molly." Greg lifted his finger to my temple.

"Thank you." We walked back to my car in silence. The cold air brushed against my cheeks. The heat in Greg's cottage must have had my cheeks on fire. "Thank you for walking me to my car. I'm sure that I would have been capable on my own."

"I know you would have been. If you haven't noticed by now, my mum raised a gentleman and if she seen you walking to your car on your own. Let me put it this way. My head would be bursting after she was finished."

I laughed, as I opened my boot for him to put my bags in. Caroline could be a funny character if she had a bee in her bonnet. "I better let you get back to Kayleigh."

"Goodnight, Molly." Greg placed a soft kiss on my cheek, as I felt his hand rest on my side, directly over my bump. I felt my heart rate pick up. My breathing was going to give me away if I didn't move.

"Goodnight, Greg." I opened my door and climbed into my car.

"Breath, Molly. Breath, Molly." I repeated that to myself a few times as I drove away.

We've both done very well until the final hurdle.

Tonight was fantastic. I had no idea that I would have so much fun.

Chapter 5

What Was That?

Greg

I let the breath out that I was holding in, from the minute Molly got in her car. I stood and watched her pull off down our driveway. I felt like I was drawn to watch her until she was out of sight.

"I think you can go home now, son." I turned around quickly to see my dad standing on his porch with a cup in his hand.

"Yeah." I looked back at the driveway and took a couple of steps backward, until I turned and walked to my dad. "You're up late."

I tried to change the subject so that he wouldn't mention Molly. My mum was bad enough, talking about my love life, or lack of it, without my dad starting.

"Final coffee before bed. How was your night?"

"It was good. A lot of ground covered."

"I bet there was."

"Dad. Molly is a friend. A very pregnant friend. Take your head out of the gutter." I took a step back to go home.

"I'm only kidding you on, son. Don't take it to heart. I'm glad to see that you had a young lady over for dinner. It is about bloody time."

"Goodnight, dad." I wasn't in any frame of mind to stand and listen to my dad.

"You think I'm bad? Just wait until your mother questions you in the morning."

I stopped listening. I just kept walking to my house. I needed a cold shower and bed. That was my plan for the rest of the night.

Before I turned all the lights out, I picked up my phone from the table. I thought of a million different reasons not to text Molly, but I couldn't help myself.

TO MOLLY:

FROM GREG:

MSG

Thank you for a lovely evening, Molly. I hope you get home ok.

Greg. Xx

I threw my phone down on my bed and proceeded to go for the cold shower. Anything to take my mind off of Molly.

Chapter 6

Moving Day

Molly

I am worked up. Not only am I moving in today, I am going to get checked over at 2 o clock. This is for the scan that I was meant to have at twenty weeks. I was in the middle of here and Aberdeen, so I didn't get the appointment. So it's nearly 4 weeks overdue and I just want to run away.

I snapped at everyone so far and it isn't even lunchtime. Greg set his men to work so they knew what was getting done, but I haven't seen *him* yet. He had some work to do at the farm, but he said he would be here at some point this afternoon.

I'm glad in a way, that I haven't seen him, because he would probably get his head bitten off as well.

Nothing was going to plan. The moving men don't give a shit, even though the boxes are marked to go in certain rooms. I put notes on the doors so they know what room is which, but I don't think they're capable of reading.

"Where do you want this? It isn't marked." I look around at the two young boys wheeling a fridge freezer in and I raise my brows before I rub my temple to ease the ache.

"Are you serious? It's a kitchen appliance, so that means it goes in the bloody kitchen!"

"Okay. Maybe I should turn around and walk out before I get something thrown at me." The minute I heard Greg's voice I relaxed...slightly.

"I can't do this!" I sat on to the step separating my living room and dining room and took a deep breath in.

The moment I sat down, Greg kneeled in front of me and rested his hand on my knee. "What's wrong, Molly?"

"All morning, it's been chaos. Not one thing has gone right. The only thing that has worked out is your bloody men. They came in and got on with what they were supposed to."

"Like I expected them to."

"Can't those goons do the same? I just had that idiot asking me where to put a fridge. A fucking fridge!" I took a few deep breaths and just stopped before I did anyone any harm.

"Okay. This is what's going to happen. I'm going to sort these movers out and I want you to go and get a cup of tea. No arguing with me. When that's done, I'm coming to find out what has really got you in this mood." He stood up and held his hands out for me to take. I was glad for his help, because my mood had me down on a step and I would have probably struggled to get up from. "Go."

I watched him head away outside to see the movers. I would have loved to be a fly on the wall, but the hot cup of tea was shouting for me more.

I didn't argue with him. I just took off toward the kitchen. The kettle is already plugged in, just waiting to get filled up. A nice cup of tea is exactly what I need. It might not do very much, but it will ease some of the stress.

"Sit down on that bar stool and I will finish this." I'm not used to taking orders, but when Greg told me what to do, I just did it.

"What did you say to those idiots out there?"

"Probably nothing much that you haven't already said."

I rested my head on the corner of my arm. I just want to get this day over with.

"What is going on Mol?" I looked into Greg's eyes, as he called me the pet name he has for me. "I am not letting you out of this kitchen until you tell me."

"I just wanted today to go without a hitch. I thought if I could get through today, then I would get through the rest of my life on my own."

"Just because a few movers tried to piss you off, doesn't mean you won't get through anything else. Has anyone else given you a hard time?"

"Apart from my dad on a phone and Sylvia, no."

"Now that's cleared up. What else is bothering you?" His body leaned over the breakfast bar in front of me reaching for my hand.

"I have to go out in the next hour and I wanted the removal guys gone."

"I can take care of them until you come back."

"I can't ask you to do that. It's a hospital appointment I am going to and they can take forever."

"Hospital? Are you okay?" I heard the concern in Greg's voice and I tried to smile to put his mind at rest, but I couldn't. I was nervous as hell about this scan.

"I should have had a 20-week scan nearly four weeks ago."

"What aren't you telling me?"

"When I had my 12 week scan, they told me the baby's head wasn't the size it should have been. They told me to have an amniocentesis, but I said no because it had a risk of miscarriage. I have put it to the back of my mind with everything going on, but now it's here I can't put it out of my mind."

"Why didn't you tell me this before now? I...you're not going alone. I'm coming with you."

"No!" I didn't want to put Greg out any more than I already have.

"It isn't up for discussion, Molly. I'm coming with you and that is that. I will tell Ross to keep those movers in check. Go and get ready."

"But..."

"No buts! Go!" I heard the snap in Greg's tone and I wasn't in the mood to argue with him today. I've done more snapping today than I have done in the last year.

I usually have a plan, but today it has gone to pot. Now I have to take control of the day and make my way to the scan.

It was time to see junior again.

***

Sitting in the hospital waiting room was making my heart race. I was fiddling with the strap of my handbag and was going to end up snapping it if I kept going.

"You're nervous and I get that, but I'm not leaving you. I'll come in if you want." Greg's voice soothed me slightly. The moment I looked into his eyes, I was like putty.

"I don't want you to be uncomfortable. I will be fine."

"I'm not saying that I'm going to be of any use in there, but I can hold your hand." His warm hand rested over mine to stop me from snapping my bag strap. I had to smile at him because he knew I loved this bag.

"Only if you're sure, Greg."

"I wouldn't have offered if I wasn't sure."

"Okay." I rested my head on Greg's shoulder and wondered what I have done to deserve a friend like him.

"Molly McGregor." I lifted my head up. Greg's hand never left mine as he encouraged me to stand.

It might have taken a few minutes for my brain and legs to connect, but I put a smile on my face and followed Greg and the midwife.

Hi, Molly. My name is Claire. I'm going to perform your ultrasound today. Now I know that this scan is late. I've got your files from Aberdeen. I also noted that the baby's head measurements were off on your last scan. Did anyone tell you why that was?"

I was about to open my mouth, when the door opened and in walked a doctor in scrubs. "They told me about having an amniocentesis, but I said no. They said that by 20 weeks it would be more apparent what was going on. They also said that it could be nothing."

"That's correct. I'm going to do the ultrasound and see what I can pick up. This is Dr. Miller. He's going to look over my shoulder while I do it. If there is nothing to worry about, then you won't have to hear from him."

All I could do was nod and smile. I let them get me ready for the scan and I felt the tears well up in my eyes. I had no idea what they were for, but I had a funny feeling that I was going to get some bad news.

Greg's hand reached over and squeezed mine. I was glad that he was here, because otherwise I would have crumbled a long time ago.

"Okay, Molly. You can look straight ahead and see everything on the screen. Once I have all the measurements, I will point everything out to you. It's always nice for mum and dad to know what they are looking at."

I felt like I should have corrected the midwife but my mouth wouldn't open. I couldn't get any words out. I was hoping that Greg would be able to correct her, but all he did was move his chair closer to me and rubbed circles on my hand with his free hand.

I felt her push and prod my tummy, but I couldn't look at the screen. I felt like I needed to know what was going on before I could look at my baby again.

"A nice strong heartbeat." The voice echoed in my head and I couldn't control the tears any longer.

Greg stood beside me and wiped my tears away.

I could hear the midwife and doctor talking away from me, but not loud enough to make out.

"Hi, Molly. I'm Dr. Miller, but you can call me Adam. Since you haven't had an amniocentesis, it's difficult for us to diagnosis anything with just an ultrasound. I'm going to run through findings with you and your partner and then we can discuss where we go from here. Okay?"

"Is he okay?" The only three words I could think of.

"From your first scan, it was hard to say what could be going on. That's why we' like to do this scan between 20-24 weeks. There are several things that I've just picked up that would indicate that your baby has some form of Down's Syndrome."

I let his words sink in but I didn't think I could breathe on my own. Greg placed a soft kiss on my head, as he continued to sooth me.

"Your baby has a decrease in the femur length. Now that's only one thing. Your baby has also got an increase in the skin behind the neck. This is called Nuchal Translucency. Unfortunately, on its own, it isn't a definite answer. When it's paired with a few issues, it can give us a clearer picture. I have also spotted a little patch of the baby's brain where there could be a Choroid Plexus Cyst. This is a little cyst on the baby's brain that produces spinal fluid. Now, these things in general won't harm your baby, but they are all signs of Down's Syndrome. I know you didn't want an amniocentesis, but maybe you would like to think about it now. We can also run some blood tests called a Triple Screen. It lets us see if there are three substances in your blood stream. This will give us another indication as to whether your baby has Down's Syndrome, or not.

"I know this is a lot to take in, but I had to tell you everything. Do you have any questions?"

I couldn't bring myself to speak. I was dumbfounded as the tears run down my face. Greg asked what I tried to. "Does Molly have to decide right now?"

"No, no, no. You can go home and talk it through. Call us when you do decide. Claire can give you her direct number."

"If I say yes to these tests, can they be done today?" I finally found my voice.

"Yes." I took a deep breath. "We can give you five minutes to yourself and we will come back. There is no rush. If you decide that you want to go home and think about it, that's fine."

The moment the doctor and midwife left us, Greg comforted me until there were no more tears left for me to cry. I knew that the doctor and midwife would be back and I haven't even said one word yet. "Talk to me, Molly. I want to help you."

"You should go home for Kayleigh."

"Not happening. My mum is getting Kayleigh her dinner tonight. I'm here with you until the end."

"I don't know what to do, Greg. I'm scared in case anything happens to my baby."

"Only you can make this decision. I can only support your decision. You deserve to have the best." I see the tears glisten in his eyes and I know exactly what he is feeling.

"If this was your baby, what would you say?" I know I had no right to ask this question, but I don't know what to do on my own. I have never felt so scared in my life.

Greg's lips placed a soft kiss on my lips and looked directly into my eyes. "If you were mine, I would have done exactly what I have done since I stepped into this hospital with you. I would have wiped your tears away and showed you love and support. If this baby was mine, I would tell you that I wouldn't care how they were born. As long as he is breathing and happy, that's all that matters. I would be there to support you no matter what. I do think the test might benefit you to get your head around it, but it isn't going to change the way you feel about this baby. You will love him or her no matter what."

Again, my tears flowed freely and I let Greg wrap me in his arms until minutes felt like hours. I knew that I had to do these tests. I had to have a definite answer now. I need to know how to care for him. I need to know that he is going to survive regardless of what disability he may or may not have.

***

We left the hospital and Greg helped me into the car. I was told to have complete bed rest for the next 24 hours, because the amniocentesis that I had done could put strain on my pregnancy. Bed rest was going to be hard, considering I was living in chaos.

We drove the entire way home in silence. It was practically dark outside and I didn't notice where we were, until we were sitting outside Greg's farm.

"What are we doing here?" I asked, as I looked around.

"You were told to rest for 24 hours, so you're staying with me until you are back on your feet."

"Greg. I am not ill."

"I knew you were going to argue this point with me, so I'll put it this way. You might not like it, but tough. You're not ill, but that baby needs rest. You might not feel ill, but putting strain and stress on your body isn't good for the baby. So, you either come in with me and stay for a couple of days, or I drop you off at Sylvia's. I already know the full story, so I won't hound you for information. Sylvia on the other hand..."

"24 hours."

"Until your house is in some order. If you're not going to do it for *you*, then do it for the baby. Let us take care of all the building work before you go back. I have a spare room here, so I would rather have you were I can see you. I'm sure Kayleigh will enjoy having you around for a little while." I smile and look out of the front windshield.

He's bloody good. He has just thrown everything at me that I can't argue with.

"We can sit here all night if you'd like, or we can go in and get some dinner and relax before bed." I punched his arm and unfastened my seat belt, before I opened the door. "What part of nothing strenuous do you not understand?"

I laugh, as I get out. He gets out and places a hand around my waist to guide me to his house.

"I have two feet that work. I am quite capable of walking to your cottage."

"Just humor me, Molly." I didn't see the point in fighting him on anything. I just wrapped my hand around his waist and let him walk me to his house. I actually quite liked to feel that close to him. I felt safe and secure when he was around.

I don't think I would have got through today without him.

***

After a nice soak in a hot bubble bath, I got out and put my pajamas on. I have no idea how he manages to get me my things while he hasn't left my side, but I wasn't complaining. It was nice to be relaxed and fresh.

I walk through to the living room and I see Greg sitting with his feet up on the coffee table. Just seeing him with a pair of shorts and white vest top on, leaves me feeling breathless.

"I think this is the first time I have seen you relax. No work. No farm. Nothing but sitting still." I tried to keep the tone light, because after the day we had, we could use some humor.

He held his hand out to me and I watched as he turned in his seat. So one leg was on the couch and the other was on the floor. I thought twice about joining him. I feel more relaxed when he is around, so I took his hand and let him place me on the couch in between his legs with my back up against his chest. His muscly arms wrapped around my shoulders and I felt my body relax into his embrace. "You feel much more relaxed tonight."

"That's all thanks to you, mister."

"I didn't do anything that any other decent guy wouldn't have done."

"Don't be so modest. There aren't many guys who would take a pregnant woman to the hospital, hold her hand all the way through, sit through tests, then bring them home and do what you are doing."

My hand was rubbing up Greg's arm, when I realized what I was doing. I didn't care. I was comfortable and felt tired enough to sleep.

"I'll be here for you any time, Molly. Before and after the baby is here. You won't get rid of me that easily." I smiled at Greg's word's, but my eyes felt so heavy as I felt them shutting.

Chapter 7

This Is The Life

Greg

My eye's flickered open and I realized that Molly and I had fallen asleep on the couch. I looked over to the clock by the fireplace and noticed it read, 4:45. I ached, so I can only imagine how soar and uncomfortable Molly is going to be when she wakes up.

I know I should be moving for work, but I am comfortable with this woman in my arms. For the first time in 6 years, I am sitting here with not a care in the world about running the farm.

"I didn't want to wake you, so I came through and got breakfast started." I jumped out of my skin, as my mum appeared from nowhere. "How is she doing?" whispered my mum, as she placed a cup of coffee down on the table.

"Surprisingly good. We fell asleep before 10 o'clock, so she is going to be sore when she gets up. I need to move to get to work. Sam will be wondering where I am."

"Don't worry about that this morning. Sam knows that you're here with Molly. He said he can take care of everything."

"Thanks, mum."

"Standing here looking at you with Molly, makes me proud of the man you have become. I hope you two realize your fate before it's too late." I looked at my mum, as she walked out of the living room.

I pulled the cover up over Molly as I tried to move, but it was a losing battle. I couldn't move without waking her.

"What time is it?"

Molly's soft voice made me still in case she was dreaming or talking in her sleep. "Have we slept here all night?"

"I was trying not to wake you. I am sorry."

"Don't be silly, Greg. You need to go to work."

"I don't actually. I have the morning off." Molly's body turned slowly toward my chest and stopped when her eyes met mine.

"Please don't change your routine because I'm here. I think I'm capable of not doing anything."

"That's just it. I know you're not capable of listening. I wouldn't even be off my porch and you would be trying to do something. I'm taking you to Sylvia's before I go to Ethel's Farm."

"Are you kidding me?" She snapped, while trying her hardest not to smile.

"Would you like a cup of tea, Molly?" my mum asked. I couldn't help but laugh when Molly jumped, when she heard my mum come back in.

"I know how you feel," I replied. "She's here every morning and even I jump when she puts a coffee down on the table."

"Mrs. Macintosh. Please don't go to any trouble. I can make a cup of tea." Molly smiled.

"Let's get some ground rules set. You can call me Caroline. A guest of Greg's is a guest of mine. If I can't make you tea and breakfast, then there is something wrong." I felt her shrink back into my arms with a smile on her face.

"You think that I'm bad?" I add. "Now you've met my mum and she won't take no for an answer."

"Now I know where you get it from," Molly said, with a grin.

I know that I love Molly, but I have to keep that to myself and keep her as a friend. I would rather have her as a friend than nothing at all.

I've spent too long on my own with Kayleigh, but now I'm having feelings for someone. I feel isolated. I don't know how to act.

The best thing I can do is just be there for Molly when she needs me.

Chapter 8

Getting There

Molly

The Last four weeks have gone by so slowly. The deeper Greg gets in, the more problems he faces. He had to replace a few walls because of mildew and it's been one nightmare after another.

I got out of the car outside my cottage and for once, it looks really quiet. Usually there are people all around, in and out and causing chaos.

I look around. Even the cottage is quiet. "Hello."

I make my way to the kitchen and place my bag down on the worktop before I inspect what has been done since the last time I was here.

I'm distracted by the sound of my phone ringing, so I take it out of my pocket. "Hello? Yes, this is Molly...Oh, right...Yes, I understand...Thank you!"

I place the phone down on the side table and lean down onto my elbows, before my legs gave way.

"Molly." I feel Greg come up behind me and wrap his arms around my waist to stop me from sinking any further. "Speak to me, Molly."

I can't bring myself to speak. I am rendered speechless again. I was expecting the call about my results, but now it has hit me right in the face and I can't breathe. "I can't breathe, Greg!"

His arms turn me around. "Open your eyes and look at me. Take deep breaths in and out. That's it. You only panicked, but you can breathe." His warm lips placed a soft kiss on my head as I burrowed myself into his shoulders.

He probably guessed what the call was, but I need to tell him anyway. "That was the hospital."

No words left Greg's mouth. I could feel his heart beating against my chest and I know he won't interrupt me. "He has got Down's Syndrome, Greg. The tests were all positive. Every single test was positive."

Again, I felt his arms tighten around me as I compose myself in his warmth. "I have something to show you," said Greg.

I pull away slowly and his hand finds mine. I was curious to see what he had to show me, because anything would be a good distraction.

I follow behind him, as he takes me along the corridor to where I am going to make the nursery. "If you don't like any of this, we can change it. I got all the furniture from Sylvia. She told me what you were planning to do with this room."

I was nervous. I want to see what Greg has been up to.

The door opens and I take a deep breath as the fresh smell of paint and carpet hit my senses. I look around and the light mint, lemon and cream hit me. The wall mural is baby animals in a rainforest. I go in and rub my hand over the cot in the middle of the room.

This has got to be the nicest thing anyone has ever done for me. It's perfect.

"It can be changed." I turn and look at Greg, leaning against the door. He looks terrified that I might not like any of this.

I walk back to him, pull his face down to me, and place a kiss on his cheek. "Greg! I love it!"

The tears start again, but this time they're happy tears.

I am going to give birth in a couple of months. I'm going to have a baby. I am going to be a mother.

Today is just the fresh start that we all need.

Chapter 9

Life Is A Bitch

Greg

Both Kayleigh and I are lost without Molly here. I was a bit upset when she said that she needed to stay at her own house after the rooms were done.

She's gotten it into her head that she has put me out long enough. How can I tell her that I love having her here? I feel complete when she is around. I never thought I would have any other woman in my house after Kayleigh's mum left us. I always told myself that my mum and my daughter are the only two women that I need in my life. I'm not so sure that I can say that now.

"Daddy. Are we going to Molly's after school? I haven't seen her for two days and I miss her."

"I'm not sure what is happening yet, but I will let you know when I pick you up from school."

"Please."

"It depends how much work we get done today. Go get all your school stuff ready. The school bus will be here in ten minutes."

I watched Kayleigh bounce out of the kitchen, happily. She is like a little ray of sunshine. "Greg. How long is this going to go on for?"

I look over at my mum loading the dishwasher, looking at me as she places each dish safely in the right place.

"I don't know what you're talking about, mum."

"You're miserable without Molly. Kayleigh misses her, too. Stop pretending that you haven't fallen in love with the girl. Do us all a favor."

"Mum. You don't know what you're talking about. Even if I do love Molly, nothing will ever come of it. She doesn't want a relationship with anyone. I'm not spoiling what we do have."

"So you're just going to sit there trying to play matchmaker?" I stood up and placed my cup on the worktop. I was getting fed up of the whole world trying to push me and Molly together.

I know that I love her. I know that I want her in more ways than just friendship, but it isn't going to happen.

Not many people can say that they have a friend like Molly. She is kind, funny, helpful, full of joy, and great with kids. Perfect in every sense.

"Mum. Can you make sure Kayleigh is on the bus? I need to do something."

"Of course I can. Will I get her off the bus as well?"

"I'll let you know at lunch time." I pick up my car keys and met Kayleigh in the hall. She was surrounded by books and papers from her bag. "What are you doing, darling?"

"I was trying to clean my bag out. Where are you going?"

"Here let me help you. I’m going to work, sweetheart. Granny is going to walk you to the bus. Have a good day." I took her in my arms and she gave me a kiss before I handed her back her bag.

If someone said to me 10 years ago that I would have a daughter, I would have thought there wasn’t a chance in hell. I wouldn't change her for the world now. "Love you, daddy."

I turn around from the front door and blow a kiss over to my little princess. "I love you too, baby."

I have to get out of this house and do what I’m going to do before I chicken out. She can only say no.

It isn't the end of the world.

Chapter 10

Just Say Yes

Molly

Sitting at my breakfast bar with the laptop open, wasn't what I expected to be doing today. I let all my work pile up this week and it all needs to be done before I get around to opening up my business.

I don't know how I can work in here with the noise. The banging is starting to get on my nerves. I'm glad that this should be the last week before the farmhouse is finished. They can all move on to the barn conversion then.

I was looking forward to some peace and quiet. The barn is far enough away from the house that I shouldn't hear much.

"Molly!" I looked at my watch the minute I heard Greg's voice. I wasn't expecting him here until this afternoon.

"I'm in the kitchen!" I shouted back.

Before I could stop what I was doing, he was pressed up against my back with his hands resting on my hips. I was a bit surprised at the welcome I was getting, because he has been pretty docile the last couple of days. "Good morning," I said, as I took my glasses off and placed them down beside my laptop.

"Morning."

"Ross said you weren't due here until this afternoon."

"Change of plans." I was kind of nervous because it isn't like him to be blunt with me. I'm used to the fun loving guy.

"Are you going to tell me, or am I going to have to guess? Can I see your face or am I not allowed to move?"

"I have something to ask you," he said, with a serious tone.

"Okay." I tapped my fingers on the surface of the bar from sheer nerves. If only I could see Greg's face, I would get a sense of what was going on. His body is rigid. "Out with it then, because you're making me nervous."

"I missed you the last couple of days. Kayleigh asked to come and see you tonight."

"You don't need to ask me if Kayleigh can come and see me. I told you she is welcome here any time. I missed her as well." I had a funny feeling that this wasn't all he was going to ask me.

"That wasn't all I wanted to ask you."

"Oh for goodness sakes Greg! Will you spit it out? Unless you've forgotten I am due to give birth in several weeks! You're scaring me!" I didn't mean to yell at him but I hated to be kept in the dark.

I tried to turn in my seat since they are swivel stools, but his hands put a little extra pressure on my sides to keep my back to him.

"I have a log cabin booked for this weekend in Aviemore. A friend of mine is in a band and I said I would go and see him. I haven't seen them for a long time and they kind of twisted my arm."

"Cool. You really deserve a break from family and work." Again, I tried to turn in my seat but was stuck in the one spot.

"My mum and dad are going to watch Kayleigh for me. Since we're finishing with the farmhouse on Friday morning, I thought you might like to join me for the weekend."

Was I hearing him right? A weekend in Aviemore? Just the two of us? Why all the heroics? "Is that why you won't let me look at you?"

"No. I just like having you in my arms. I missed your cuddles on the couch the last two nights."

"So, this weekend. What do you have planned?"

"Not a lot," he replied. "I thought it might be your last break before the baby comes along, so we can have a quiet weekend."

"What's the catch?" I asked, cheekily. I know there isn't any other motive, but I hate the seriousness.

"Apart from me getting to spend the weekend with a gorgeous woman, I have nothing else to gain from this. Just say yes, Molly."

"I don't know, Greg." As much as I wanted to go with him to Aviemore, I didn't want to give off mixed signals. I know we're getting closer, but we haven't grown as close as I would like.

"It's a weekend away, Molly. Two friends having some fun. Nothing more. Nothing less."

I was surprised when I was allowed to turn. My eyes met with Greg's rock solid chest and I followed his body up until I met his eyes.

"When do we leave?" I asked, quietly.

"Friday. I'll pick you up and I'll do the driving." His soft lips placed a kiss on the end of my nose and then he turned away from me. I looked at Greg's back wondering what was going on. Was that all he came to ask me?

"Before I forget, don't cook tonight. I'll pick you up at 5pm. I thought we could go for a pizza with Kayleigh. It seems that she is having withdrawal symptoms from seeing you."

"Okay."

I know that I was crazy to agree to this, but we both deserve a nice weekend away and Kayleigh deserves to have what she wants. If that means a couple of hours in Pizza Hut, then so be it.

What harm can it do?

***

Sitting in a booth in Pizza Hut on a Wednesday teatime, with kids running back and forth to the ice cream factory would never have been my idea of fun. However, things have changed dramatically and I can actually laugh at their excited faces getting high on sugar.

"How did you two know that I wanted to come to Pizza Hut?" asked Kayleigh, as she took a big bite of pizza.

"A wee birdie told me," said Greg making his daughter laugh.

"I'm not a baby any more, daddy. You can't tell me that birds talk and expect me to believe it."

I was laughing now, too. "Well young lady, some birds do talk. Parrots talk," Greg said, with a grin.

"Yeah, but you didn't say a parrot. You said a bird," Kayleigh responded with a serious look.

"You're digging yourself a deeper hole, Greg," I said, with a smirk.

"Is it gang up on dad day?"

"Wait until the baby arrives and he joins my side," said Kayleigh.

I had to smile in Greg's direction, because her little mind has worked through every scenario and came up with a plan.

I was overwhelmed that she was including my baby in her shenanigans. It was going to be interesting to see him taking the piss out of Greg, along with Kayleigh.

"I think I'll just sit here and not say another word," joked Greg, as he winked in my direction."

"Can I get ice cream now?" asked Kayleigh.

"Oh, you want to talk nice to me now that you want something?" he asked, while tickling his daughter and making her giggle. "Of course, you can get ice cream."

"She has a fantastic nature," I said, watching her as she got further away from us.

"She's crazy," he returned.

"I wonder where she gets that from, Mr. Macintosh?"

"Oh, is that right? I'll get you back." I laughed at Greg as he realized that I was on Kayleigh's side. He now knew that he's going to get it from both sides of the table, so he was as well just accepting it.

CHAPTER 11

Break Away

Molly

After a Crazy two months of trying to get my life in order, I feel like I need this weekend away. When Greg told me that he has a friend who has a cottage in Aviemore, I was surprised to find out that he wanted me to go with him.

Of course, I had to think clearly about this. I don't want to ruin our friendship, so I tried to say no, but Greg had it all worked out.

The final straw was when he told me this could be my last weekend away before the baby is born. I only have eight weeks left and I'm terrified of becoming a single mum. I have tried to ease my mind by telling myself, if Greg can be a great single dad, then I can be a great single mum.

I know it's going to be hard, but life is hard. Nothing in this world is easy. I'll just do everything in my power to make everything work out perfectly.

This weekend is a must for us both. We can go up to Aviemore and relax in the cold winter air. I was looking forward to it, because I haven't done something spontaneous like this for years.

"Molly!" I heard Greg's voice echo from downstairs in my hallway. "Are you ready?"

"I'm upstairs! Come up and help me!" I shouted down to him.

He has perfect timing as always. It doesn't matter when I need him, he just seems to appear.

I don't know why I'm so comfortable around Greg. I would never usually ask for help. I would have struggled with my case until he came to my aid.

"Hey, gorgeous." I felt the heat rise in my cheeks. You would think I would be used to it after knowing Greg for several months. It might be a short time to some, but I feel like I have known him my whole life.

"Hi, yourself." I stood up straight and lifted the handle on my suitcase.

"Ready?" He asked, as I looked around my room.

"I'm ready if you are."

"We're only going for a weekend, Molly. Have you left anything at home?" he teased, as he took my case away from me.

"I left the kitchen sink," I joked back.

"It is a good thing I'm taking the Jeep with us." We were like an old married couple some days.

"Stop your moaning and just get on with it, before I change my mind and stay at home." I was playfully trying to shut him up.

One thing I love about spending time with Greg, was the simple fact that we had fun. We were two people just having fun together. Our friendship has grown over the last several weeks and I love him and Kayleigh like family.

"I need to stop at Sylvia's to hand in my keys. My dad is coming down on Sunday and Sylvia is going to look after the dogs until I get home."

"No problem at all. Are you ready to leave now?" he asked, impatiently.

"Sure. The dogs have food and water until Sylvia comes over." Gizmo came bounding through the hall and jumped up for my legs, until I crouched down and showed him some attention. I love having my two pugs here with me now. They make it feel like home. "You be a good boy until granny Sylvia comes over."

We got out onto my front porch and I locked my door. The cold winter air just hit me and I desperately wanted to get into the car for heat. Greg's Jeep was nice with heated seats. Something I never thought I would like before. I reached the car, as Greg was climbed into the driver's seat. I'm glad that he stopped opening my door for me after I told him that I was more than capable of doing it myself. I know he is a gentleman and it is in his nature to make sure I am okay, but I can do it myself.

I looked around, just to make sure that nothing was out of place before we took off on our journey.

It was crazy to think how much has been done in just a couple of months. I was blessed to be comfortable in a place that I have come to love. This is now my home. A home that is coming along nicely.

That was my last thought about home. I was just going to sit back and enjoy the relaxation.

"It is bloody freezing," I said, as I rubbed my hands together. The heat from the car immediately hit me, which made me happy.

"Wait until we reach Aviemore. It will be even worse." I rolled my eye's because although I am moaning about the cold weather, I know that Aviemore always get weather ten times worse than we do.

"I was a child the last time I was up in Aviemore. It was late December or early January, but it was lovely. In a winter kind of way," I said, reminiscing.

"We're nearly a month early, but I am sure it will be just as nice at the beginning of December." I don't doubt anything Greg has to say. I know that he would do everything in his power to make this weekend enjoyable.

"Was Kayleigh okay about staying with your parents?" I asked, changing the subject.

"She was, in the end. I had to give her twenty pounds for a new computer game." I had to laugh at Greg being conned by such a sweet little girl. She really did have her dad wrapped around her little finger.

"She could have been with us, you know. I would have loved to have her here."

"I know. I also know that you're great with her, but I wanted to be selfish for once and have you all to myself. You have been through so much the last couple of months and I wanted to do something relaxing for you, before the baby arrives."

"I don't know what I have done to deserve a friend like you, but I'm so happy I found you. It's been a tough couple of months, but I got through it all. Thanks to you."

I usually don't act all soppy, but Greg has helped me with the house and barn conversion. He was there when I found out that my baby has Down's Syndrome. He has just been a complete support blanket for me and I will never be able to thank him enough.

"Molly. I'm glad that I found you, too. I will always be here for you and the baby. No matter what." His warm hand reached over and squeezed my hand that was resting on my leg.

"You are the only person that hasn't felt sorry for me with the news about the baby. I need that from you. I don't think I would have been so strong if it wasn't for your support."

"Molly. I didn't feel sorry for you, because I know that this won't make any difference to you. You're going to love your baby no matter what and I will be here to offer any support that I can."

Greg pulled up outside Sylvia's B&B and turned to me. His warm hand rested on my cheek and I felt comfortable with him yet again. A couple of months ago I would have pulled away, so I've come a long way.

"We're going to Aviemore for the weekend and I don't want you to worry about anything. I'm not asking you to forget about the last couple of months, but I am asking you to put it to the back of your mind. I have a few surprises this weekend and I hope you like them." His soft tone sent goosebumps through my body.

"You have surprises for me?" I asked.

"I do. Are you going into Sylvia's so we can get this weekend started?" He leaned over and kissed me gently. I felt a smile spread across my face. I was getting used to the soft kisses.

I pulled away to open the door and I couldn't believe that Greg was going to all of this bother for me. I never had a friend like him before and I was blessed to have him in my life.

He had me intrigued to find out what he has in store for me this weekend.

***

"Molly." I opened my eyes slowly to realize that I had fallen asleep on our journey to Aviemore. "We're there, sleepy head."

I leaned forward and looked around. It was nearly dark and the snow was sparkling on the ground. "I'm sorry, Greg. I meant to take a shot of driving."

"I told you that I could manage the driving. It isn't like you're in any state to drive."

"Excuse me?" I raised my brows and smiled. "I thought we got over this on our first meeting. I'm pregnant, not ill." I tried to keep a playful tone.

"Eight months pregnant to be exact, Molly."

"Eight months pregnant. Hungry and needing to stretch my legs," I huffed. I wanted to get out of the car to see where we're staying.

"I have made a reservation down at the local pub for dinner at 7pm. It gives us time to freshen up." I should have known that Greg would have everything organized.

"You seem to have everything very well organized, mister." I leaned over and opened my door. My boots crunched down into the snow. I was glad that I decided to wear my Ugg boots, because anything else and I would no doubt land on my backside. "It is beautiful."

I fell asleep in the car with my jacket on, so now I can feel the cold air immediately hit me.

I turned to see where Greg was standing and the little cottage was so beautiful. The Cottage is situated along rolling hills near a quiet lane that leads to open countryside. The delightful single story cottage has been upgraded and refurbished to provide bright and cozy accommodations. With the town just a few minutes away, I was now like a child at Christmas.

I crunched through the snow and Greg held his hand out to me, so that I wouldn't fall. I was glad to take his hand, because I didn't want to end up on my bum or in a hospital.

The moment the front door opened, the heat hit us. I was glad that it was nice and cozy.

We headed into the main living room and the open fire was blazing. The cottage was dimly lit with extra light coming from a lamp in the corner. The fire had the whole room glowing. I was stunned to see how lovely it was.

"I hope you like it," he said, placing both hands on my shoulders. It was like a picture out of a magazine.

"Greg..." I turned around slowly to take in the rest of the room and I came eye to eye with this beautiful, warm-hearted man. For the first time since I met him, I could see his eyes sparkling at me. "Thank you, for bringing me here."

"My pleasure." I suddenly got the feeling that Greg was struggling to say exactly what he wanted to. The silence between us wasn't golden. I just wanted the chatty Greg back with me. "Molly..."

"Greg..."

We both said each other's name at the same time, as our soft laughter filled the cottage. It was like being back at school again, about to kiss my first boyfriend behind the bike sheds. I suddenly felt my cheeks flush.

"I don't want to ruin this weekend before it even begins, but I need to tell you something, Molly. I can't let another day go by without telling you."

I felt nervous. I felt the butterflies flutter through my stomach.

"Why don't we start again? Why don't we put the light on and...?" I went to switch the light on but Greg's soft hand caught my wrist to stop me. "Maybe not."

"Molly. I think it's obvious that we both have feelings for one another. I know that we said that we would be friends for Kayleigh and the baby's sake, but I am struggling. I see your heart breaking every day and I want to take your pain away. I want to hold you and let you see that everything is going to be okay."

"You do make everything okay, Greg." Every day he does something that makes my life more bearable.

"Not as friends, Molly. I want more. I want us to be happy together. Kayleigh has never taken to another woman before you."

"Greg, please. I can't hear this right now. I'm eight months pregnant. My hormones are all over the place. You don't want to be tied down with another man's child. A baby with Downs is going to take up all of my time."

"You're not listening to me, Molly. I don't *just* want you. I want to help you with the baby. I want to take on the responsibility of raising this baby with you." His hand rested on my stomach. I waited a long time for someone to care for the baby and me. I desperately wanted this baby to have a daddy.

I looked down at his hand, as the tears fell freely from my eyes. I couldn't hold them in even if my life depended on it. "I've wanted someone to say this and mean it. I wanted someone like you in my life, but I can't tie you down. You would hate me for it and I would rather have your friendship as opposed to nothing at all."

Silence fell between us, but Greg's hand never moved. His thumb moved slowly over my stomach and suddenly the baby kicked his hand. As much as I wanted to run, I had to smile.

"You're the only one hiding from this, Molly. Even this little one thinks we should be together."

"He likes when I rub my stomach, so he probably thought it was me." I was being childish. I was preventing myself from being happy.

"You can run from this, Molly, but you can't hide. I'm not going to give up."

"I'm going to get freshened up." I needed to leave before I caved in.

"I'll get your case from the car." His soft lips placed a tender kiss on my lips. Nothing invasive, but enough to let me see that he meant every word he just said.

He backed slowly out of the room. The moment he was out of sight, my hand came up to my mouth. My thumb rubbed against my lips, because they felt like they were throbbing from his kiss. The electric currents were flowing through my body and I didn't know why I was feeling like this.

This was going to be a long weekend.

It was going to take everything I had not to give into my feelings. I can’t deny my happiness much longer.

***

After a shower and change of clothes, I am ready for dinner. My mind hasn't stopped replaying Greg's words, but I need to get through this weekend.

I need to put a brave face on and not let him see that I want him as much as he wants me. If he opens his eye's wide enough, he will see that we will be better as friends. We are perfect together as friends and I don't want to lose him from my life.

I take in a deep breath and slowly walk through to the heart of this lovely cottage. After Greg's bombshell when we first arrived, I haven't had a chance to take in my surroundings.

"Yes, darling, but just you remember to be good for gran and grandad." I realized quickly that Greg was talking to Kayleigh, so I sat at the bar stool at the breakfast bar. The stools are handy when you are heavily pregnant. It’s easier to step off a seat, as opposed to stand up out of one.

"Is Kayleigh okay?" I asked, the moment he came off his call.

I felt Greg coming up from behind me. He placed his mobile phone down on the table and took a deep breath. He leaned down onto his elbows and rested his chin in his hands. "You seem stressed, Greg."

"I'm good. So is Kayleigh. I'm sure she is going to give my mum and dad a run for their money, but I warned her to be good."

"You should have brought her." I lost count how many times I have said this. "I know she wanted to come this weekend."

"That's why she is being a little witch, because she didn't get her way. I know my daughter better than she knows herself, and her being a brat won't get her anywhere." I couldn't stop smiling at Greg, because even when he tried to sound strict, he was like a big, soft tiger.

"Strict dad alert," I giggled, making him laugh with me.

"You'll be the same when your little one is Kayleigh's age."

"Maybe." I looked down at my hands resting on the table in front of me. It dawned on me that I won't know what I will be like as a mother. I thought I might be a strict mum, but knowing that my baby has Down's Syndrome, I think I will be a soft touch. My baby's life will be difficult enough without me barking out orders.

"Are you okay, Molly?"

"I'm fine," I tried to say confidently

"I think we're passed the stage of you lying to me. I think I can tell when you have something on your mind."

"I keep forgetting that you're good at reading me, Greg." I sat up straight and took in a deep breath myself. I was hoping that we could just go for dinner and forget about this conversation. Greg isn't going to move and there is no point in lying, because he can see right through me.

"I always see myself as being a strict mum with rules and regulations but knowing that my baby has Down's syndrome, I can't imagine myself being strict."

"Molly. Your little one is going to be like any other child. Granted she is going to have some problems, but she will be like any other happy child."

I found myself looking through Greg's eyes. It dawned on me that he is the only one who treats my baby normally.

"You think it's a girl?" I asked.

At all of my scans, they asked me if I wanted to know the gender, but I wanted it to be a surprise.

"I think it is, but it's nicer to say *she* instead of *it*."

"Can we go to dinner before I start eating you, Greg?"

The minute I finished my sentence, I felt my cheeks blush. Only I could say something ridiculous like that. Greg's hand took mine, as he finished laughing at me.

"Did your mum ever tell you that it is rude to laugh at a lady?"

"I'm sure she did, Molly, but I didn't think I was with a lady." I slapped his arm playfully, as he locked up our cottage.

The cold winter air hit me. The cold temperatures made the ground very icy.

Everything looks the same covered in snow. I can remember when I was younger and I watched the snow falling from the window. My mum always used to say the same thing on the first snowfall of the year. *“Snow is like kindness. It beautifies everything it covers.”*

"It really is beautiful up here. I don't know why it’s taken me years to return."

"I usually come up in the winter months. I brought Kayleigh up here last year to see the reindeer."

"I can't wait to bring my little one to places like this." My hand rubbed gently on my tummy through my jacket.

"Maybe next December we can bring your little bundle of joy and Kayleigh here. If you fancy getting away, I've heard Christmas is lovely here."

"I was here once for Christmas. I can remember carol singers and mince pies. We saw Santa going through the village on his sleigh. It really was magical." My eyes became misty, as I reminisced.

"It sounds wonderful. I’ll see if we can book the cottage again. I can't see it being a problem though."

I love that Greg is trying to include the baby and me in his plans for next year. I have a funny feeling that my friends and family are going to disappear slowly when my baby arrives, so it would be good to have Greg in my life as a friend.

We went slowly through town, until we stopped outside the pub where we were going to eat. The Old Bridge Inn.

As we entered, the heat from the roaring log fire hit us. The cozy atmosphere was welcoming. It was perfect, because it was also not crowded.

I followed Greg to the bar, but I held back and let him do the talking. I was too busy taking in my surroundings. The older men around the bar were all laughing and joking. Everyone seemed happy and care free.

Greg's hand took mine again and I followed him and our waitress to our table. I was excited when I saw that we were sitting to the side of the log fire. I don't know what my fascination is with open fires, but I do love them.

"Thank you," said Greg, as he took my jacket for me.

"Can I get you both a drink?" asked our elderly waitress.

"Can I be a pest and get a pot of tea please?" I know I was in a pub, but I wasn't in any state to drink alcohol and I needed a hot drink to heat me up.

"You're not being a pest, my dear. You would be surprised how many pots of tea I make in a day." I smiled at the waitress for her reassurance. It was nice to know she wasn't going out of her way.

"Can I have a pint of lager please?" asked Greg.

"Any in particular?"

"Do you have Budweiser?"

"Sure, sweetheart." I was glad to see him letting his hair down. He works too hard to not have a pint occasionally.

"Something smells delicious. Have you been here before?" I asked, before I contemplated what I was going to order.

"Whenever I visit here, I come here to eat. Everything is delicious." I was so hungry, felt like I could eat a scabby horse.

"Here we go, love," said the waitress, as she placed our drinks down. "I should have said that the soup today is lentil and bacon."

"I think I will have soup," said Greg, taking a drink of his pint.

"Yeah, me too. Can I also have steak pie, but with mashed potatoes?"

"Of course. Good choice."

" I think I'll go with a surf and turf." My eyes were locked on Greg, as he sat relaxed and care free.

"How would you like your steak cooked?"

"Well done."

"Thank you," she said, taking the menus out of our way. I was glad that we were at a restaurant that did home cooking.

I had a funny feeling that tonight was going to be a good night.

***

"Goodnight, you two," said the waitress.

I linked my arm through Greg's arm, as we got up to leave. "Goodnight. Thank you for the lovely hospitality. I guess I should be thanking you for a lovely evening as well, mister."

When we walked outside, fresh snow was falling. It was like a scene from a Christmas movie.

"I was glad to see you enjoying yourself after the bombshell I dropped on you tonight." I stilled as Greg spoke, but I knew that we would have to talk at some point.

I took in a deep breath of fresh air and rested my other hand over his arm. "It's hard not to have fun with you, Greg. In a normal world, we would be perfect together. We just have to accept what it is. We have other people to consider and we will be better off as friends."

"If that's what you want, Molly, then I support your decision. I might feel bruised and battered for a couple of days, but I love you enough to accept what you say."

His hands took mine, but I let them go and reached up to place a soft kiss on Greg's lips. It was only supposed to be a light peck on the lips, but the moment our lips touched, I felt the fireworks go off.

His hands rested on my waist, as we explored each other's mouths. I knew the right thing to do was pull away, but I couldn't.

My heart was pounding and I was sure that Greg could hear it. I moved my hands to rest on his chest and pulled away slowly to catch my breath. I tried to stop myself from crying.

I felt overwhelmed. I don't know if it was because I was tired, or if it was my hormones getting the better of me. I only knew that I had to apologize for what just happened.

I felt Greg's lips place a soft kiss on the top of my head and I slowly looked up to see the snow falling faster all around us. I held my hand out to catch the snowflakes.

"Greg. I'm so sorry. I shouldn't have..." His hand came up to my face and placed a finger over my lips. I felt like I needed to finish, but on the other hand I was glad that I didn't need to finish quite so quickly.

"Don't apologize, Molly. I know you didn't mean for that to happen. I know it wasn't supposed to go that far and I know it can never happen again. I know where I stand with you. Let's get home before one of us ends up with pneumonia."

I felt the tears start to form and I was willing them to stay locked away until I was in my room.

I felt ridiculous for feeling like a hormonal wreck. I guess in a normal situation, a pregnant woman has her partner or husband for the emotional support throughout her pregnancy. Was it bad of me to want Greg in that way?

Was it bad of me to need Greg?

This weekend was stirring emotions inside of me that I want to exist.

***

Sitting at the breakfast bar at 6am with a cup of tea in my hands, should be illegal on a Saturday morning in Aviemore.

The hours have been long.

By the time Greg and I got home last night, it was midnight. We went to our separate rooms and I stared at the ceiling for the biggest part of the night. I needed tea and I needed to get up before my legs cramped up.

Nursing the warm cup in my hands with only the soft light from the fire lighting the heart of this cottage, was relaxing. Even after events that unfolded last night, I feel warm and relaxed.

"Molly! Are you okay?" I lifted my head around to see Greg joining me in the open plan kitchen area. "You should be sleeping."

"Should be. Can’t."

"Is the baby okay?" I never thought four simple words could have my heart jumping from my chest.

"Yeah, I just couldn't sleep. I thought it would be better to get up and have a cup of tea. Sorry if I disturbed you."

"Don't be silly. I got up to use the bathroom. I thought I heard movement, so I checked it out. I didn't expect you to be sitting here though."

"The joys of feeling fat and not being able to get comfortable." I didn't want the silence to be there between us. I wanted us to be normal with one another. If a kiss was going to break up our friendship, I would never forgive myself.

"I bet I can help you fall asleep," he said, with a grin. I raised my eyes and hoped that he would elaborate. "Do you trust me, Molly?"

I bit my lip. Then I shook my head and removed the nervous thoughts from my head. This was Greg. Why the hell was I being nervous?

"Greg. Of course, I trust you. I just don't know what you can do that will help me sleep."

"You look exhausted. Come with me." His hand took mine and he helped me down off of the barstool.

"Where are you taking me?" We got out into the hall. Our rooms are right across the hall from one another.

"Pick a room."

"Mine," I said, without thinking. I was playing the game with him.

He opened my door and walked in like it was his room. He pulled the covers down on my bed and signaled for me to get in. I don't know where my courage came from, because I did exactly what he told me to.

I got in and he pulled the covers up over me. He turned off the big light. I couldn't see him, until I felt his muscular body climb into bed beside me. His arm reached out to me and my head rested on his chest. I could hear the gentle beat of his heart against my ear and I felt relaxed. His other hand rested softly over the side of my bump.

I couldn't help but think how some men would run a mile before lying next to a woman who was carrying another man's baby, but it didn't faze Greg in the slightest.

"Now try to get some sleep, Molly." His soft words echoed through my ears, as he placed a soft kiss on the top of my head.

I was surprised at how comfortable I felt. I expected to hate feeling so close to any man, but I was just kidding myself.

My eyes started to feel heavy, to the sound of his beating heart became my very own lullaby.

Try to get some sleep, Molly.

***

As my eyes slowly opened, I knew I was alone. I quickly realized that my bed was empty, but I was cuddled into the pillow Greg was sleeping on. I felt empty without him beside me. I rolled over and immediately I could smell bacon and eggs cooking. I could really get used to being pampered.

I managed to tear myself out of the warm bed and throw on my housecoat and slippers. It was amazing how cold these cottages can get in the winter. I can't imagine what it's like for people sleeping in tents and igloos in the freezing temperatures.

My stomach was beginning to betray me. I have done nothing, but eat since we arrived. Greg knows that I actually do have to eat for two.

I made my way to the kitchen and the different aromas hit my senses. I felt like I had died and gone to Heaven. I wanted food and I wanted it now!

"Something smells good. Am I in the right cottage?" I joked, as I sat down.

"I knew nothing would come between a pregnant lady and her morning meal. If I want to drag you off for the day, then you will need a good hearty Scottish breakfast inside you." I looked at him with surprise, because I was curious to know what he had planned for us.

"Dragging me away? Where do you think you're taking me today?"

"I have tickets for a Scottish band tonight. My friend is in it. You've probably heard of Skerryvore. Right?" His friend that he told me about is in Skerryvore.

"Are you kidding? Who hasn't heard of Skerryvore?" My brother loves this band. I was brought up in Aberdeen, so we used to hear a lot of Scottish music.

"I thought we could go off to see the Reindeer Centre today. What better place to visit in Aviemore?"

"Sounds great!" I didn't realize how excited I must have sounded, but his face said it all. It would be nice to do something casual today. It might actually stop me from thinking crazy thoughts about this relationship.

All I can think about is destroying this breakfast. It isn't coming quick enough for me. The smell is killing me. Even my little acrobat inside me was trying to do summersaults. "Is there anything you don't like? I have bacon, square sausage, black pudding, haggis, eggs, tattie scones, mushrooms, and tomatoes."

"Sounds great! Everything but the tomatoes."

"A lady that isn't afraid of eating decent food?" he added, as I poured orange juice from the jug sitting beside me. I smelled the bittersweet oranges.

"I don't think I can class myself as a lady, but I think you know me well enough to know that I love my food."

"The kettle just boiled, if you prefer tea, Molly."

"No, this is perfect. If I didn't know better, I would have thought you were up at the crack of dawn to prepare all of this."

"I've only been awake about an hour. I was going to bring you breakfast in bed, but you spoiled the surprise."

I don't deserve to be pampered. I don't deserve any kindness from him at all.

"Sorry that I spoiled your surprise, Greg. The smell of food cooking had this little one moving inside me."

I felt like I would make a good Santa, with the way I looked. Give me the suit and the beard and no one would tell the difference. I was looking forward to the end of this pregnancy. It has been a long 8 months and I can't wait to feel normal again.

"Here we go, your majesty." I loved Greg's playful attitude. Even after everything between us, he never seems to change. His ex was a fool to let him go.

"Why thank you, sir."

"Enjoy a good hearty Scottish farmer's breakfast." Greg parked his bum right across from me at the breakfast bar.

"If this is what you eat every day, you should be the size of a house."

"Growing up, my mum had this all cooked for us going to school. Our friends used to call in for us, because she would have rolls, bacon, and sausage waiting for them. Now she just cooks for fun. At 10am every morning, we have a breakfast break on the farm. My mum has this all cooked and placed out for us all to help ourselves. I'm a farmer's son and we are meat lovers, but it gets boring after a while."

"So you decide to cook it for me today? I would have been just as happy with toast and jam or scrambled eggs. You didn't need to go to this much bother."

"It really is no bother, Molly. It's traditional, when you are on holiday to have a cooked breakfast in the morning." He smiled as he talked.

If you were Scottish, it would be normal to eat your weight in food at any time of the day. One thing I grew up to was home cooked food and plenty of it. My gran and my mum were happiest when they were slaving in a kitchen cooking for the whole family. Cooking has never been something that I love to do, but I don't mind cooking now.

"I should have brought you here weeks ago, because it really is nice to see you relaxed and eating well." I took in Greg's words and listened to him, while I chewed my sausage.

"It's good to be away from builders, joiners, and other tradesmen floating around my farm," I said, with a sigh of relief.

"You never said farmers or architects, so I should be honored."

"You should be, Greg. You're the only one that I haven't had a heated discussion with." Well, not heated about work.

"I don't fancy getting on the wrong side of you, Molly, so I'll keep being a crawler."

" Anyone would think I was some kind of ogre, Greg."

"You're pregnant. You're allowed to be an ogre. Just don't make a habit of it."

One thing about being around Greg, is that I enjoy the way he makes me smile all the time. Just sitting here eating breakfast, makes me smile. The muscles in my face are going to ache by the time I get home, if he keeps it up.

"Let your smile change the world but don't let the world change your smile." My mum always made sure we knew this quote when we were growing up, especially if we weren't too happy about something. I was smiling, but I wasn't ready for taking that next step with Greg.

What was I waiting for?

***

"Are we all ready for a day of fun?" asked Greg, as he picked up the car keys from the coffee table.

" I can't wait! I feel a little bit more human after a shower. Your breakfast nearly put me into a coma." I wrap my scarf around my neck and wait for his witty response, but he just has a big smile plastered on his face, while he opens the door for me.

I've been looking forward to this weekend, spending the day with reindeer. I'm been like a child in a sweetie shop.

I got a sense of Deja Vu, because I did this trip with my parents. This time next year, I will be able to do the same thing with my baby boy or girl. I was just a big kid at heart. I know I have my good upbringing to thank for the way I will be with my child. The only one thing I never dreamed of happening, was raising my child alone. I want the 2.4 children and perfect house with the white picket fence. I'll have all of that minus a daddy and a husband.

***

Pulling up outside The Cairngorm Reindeer Park, everything looks magical. It's packed with families having fun in December and getting ready for Santa Claus making his yearly visit.

I must admit that Aviemore is the perfect getaway for restoring a child's belief in Santa. The snow was still falling all around us and the ground was crunching below our feet.

We're all wrapped up, as we make our way through the parking lot to the entrance of the deer park. Greg takes my hand and I feel content with his touch. I really hate how my head is telling me to do one thing, but my heart is screaming for the complete opposite.

I hate making decisions. I know what the best thing to do is, but I always let my heart overrule my head.

I keep going back to my mum. If she was alive, this would be one occasion that she would tell me to get a grip! Greg could be the best thing that has ever happened to me. She would also tell me that I need a man like him in my life and not to let past experiences put me off from getting my happily ever after.

I can hear her voice ringing in my ears as if she is standing beside me.

"Molly? Are you okay?" asked Greg, breaking my chain of thought.

"Sorry. I was a million miles away." I hated how Greg always caught me out when I was in a distant world.

"You don't have to apologize. I care about you. I don't like how you go distant with me, especially when we've had a great morning together. I know I put a lot pressure on you this weekend, but I don't want to ruin our friendship."

I take a deep breath and look around. I spot an empty corner where I drag Greg over to, without any explanation.

"Molly?"

"Just be quiet and listen to me." His cheeky smile, shows me that he's impressed with my forward attitude. "When I go off to another place, it isn't because of you. I can hear my mum telling me the truth and it just gets me in a little bit of a spin."

"Your mum had passed away. Right?"

"She has. I'm not going crazy. I can just hear the advice that she would be giving me if she was alive." I take a deep breath and run my hand through my hair to move it out of my eyes.

"Okay," he said, looking rather confused.

"I know the whole world is telling me to give you a chance. I know I should. I really should." I trail off and lower my head. I'm hoping that the answers will jump out of me.

"Molly. I didn't bring you up here to make you upset. I want to be in your life. I'm not going to force you into anything. You know that I love you with all my heart, but I'm not telling you anything you don't already know. I would do anything for you and the baby and I will be here when you sort your head out. Okay?"

"I don't deserve you," I practically whispered.

"Hey! Don't ever say that! You deserve more than I could ever give you, but I know you need to think about the baby." I hate it when he's so understanding. It would be so much easier, if he screamed and shouted at me.

"I wish I met you years ago. I wish things were simple. I wish this was your baby, but it's not." I nodded and I felt a bit of relief getting it off my chest.

"I wish all of that, too. It doesn't mean anything has to be different between us. We're here together now and we're going to enjoy the rest of our weekend." Greg said softly.

"Sounds good to me, Mr. Macintosh."

Greg's arms wrapped me in a warm embrace. Instead of it being a friendly hug, I let my head fall against his neck to feel the warmth and comfort radiating from him.

This was a feeling that I wasn't sure I could live without, but I wasn't brave enough to take a leap.

Why does everything have to be so difficult? Why can't life be simple? I could go on all day asking these questions, but it isn't going to change anything.

***

Today has been an amazing day. I know many of my friends would laugh at me for being here looking at reindeer, while being pregnant, but just to be here with someone that I connect with is an even bigger bonus.

I would never have blamed Greg for being off with me. The fact that he has been mature enough to still have a good time, just shows what an amazing person he is.

We walked non-stop all day. The weather has been snowy and cold, but that just added to the magical atmosphere.

"Thank you for today," I said, as we walked across the parking bays in the car park.

When we arrived earlier today, the entire place was packed with families. Now all the stragglers are left.

"It should be me thanking you, Molly," said Greg, still clutching my gloved hand in his.

"How do you work that one out, Mr. Macintosh?" I asked, cheekily nudging him with my hip, careful that I didn't lose my footing and make us both land on the ground.

"I wouldn't have blamed you for running last night when I dropped that bombshell on you. I just wanted you to know my true feelings. I thought if you knew, you could make your mind up."

"Where would I run to?" I joked, just to stop him from torturing himself. "It isn't like I drove up here. I certainly am not in any position to run for busses or trains."

"I'm glad, because we wouldn't have had a lovely day if you left me standing by myself." Laughter erupted from me as I thought about the last 24 hours.

If I laughed any more today, I would give birth in Aviemore.

"What's so funny?" He knew what I was laughing at.

"I pictured myself running for public transport while I'm like a beached whale and you either standing with your pride hurt, or running after me. Whatever the outcome, it would all make a good candid camera moment." I laughed, snorting, causing my eyes to water from giggling so much.

"You have a very sick sense of humor, young lady. I’m not sure that I can tolerate your tone anymore."

We were now both in fits of laughter. I always dreamed that one day I would grow old with a man that I could laugh with.

"I think you're a bad influence on me, Mr. Macintosh."

"Is that so?" said Greg, pulling me around to face him.

I felt my heart pounding and my palms were sweating through my gloves. I wanted to move, but I was intrigued to see how far I could let this go on. "Why don't you take a walk on the wild side with me, Molly?"

"What do you have in mind?" I felt my words tumble out of my mouth, as his hand stroked my cheek and he held me in place.

"We need to go home to get ready for dinner and Skerryvore," he said, quietly.

I completely forgot that we were going to see Greg's friends perform. How could I forget? It just so happens that his friends are in a very successful Scottish band that I really like.

"More excitement," I barely managed to whisper.

Greg's face moved a few inches away from me. He leaned in so close to me that I could feel the heat from his breath skim my face.

"Let's get you in the car, before you catch a cold," he said, as he moved to open his car door for me.

Yeah, it was safe to say that he just got his own back on me for playing him like a bat and ball this weekend.

I climbed into the passenger's seat without showing my disappointment. But I really felt disappointed that he didn't kiss me. I could blame it on my hormones but there was only so much blame that I could blame them for. I'm confused. I keep saying we're just friends, yet here I am complaining that he didn't kiss me.

I needed to get a grip.

I'm giving off mixed signals. I don't know whether to laugh or cry.

I'm a mess.

My pregnancy has been getting all of the blame, but I can't keep using that as an excuse. In a few short weeks, I'm going to be a mummy. My feelings are not going to matter, because my bundle of joy will be my number one priority.

That was a scary thought.

***

Today has been an emotional day. At the highest point. I felt like I was floating on a cloud. At my lowest point, I still felt like I was floating on a cloud.

After finishing dinner at the little Inn, I feel like I'm so overwhelmed.

Since Greg's little display of affection in the parking lot, he's been distant. He's still talking away, but it's like there's a glass panel between us.

"You haven't fully told me how you know the Skerryvore guys." I tried to keep the chat casual and flowing, because he wasn't keeping the conversation going.

"I went to university with Alex, the singer." I watched him take a drink of his pint and I needed to know what changed. I'm getting a reply to my answers but that's it. Nothing more.

I'm quite taken aback, because I don't usually have to ask for more details.

"Okay. I might regret saying this, but we can't go on with this atmosphere between us. I'll go back to the cottage and you can go have a good night with your friends."

I gave him a chance to answer me before I went any further. I was hoping that he would tell me to stop being silly, but there was nothing but silence between us.

I reached into my bag and took out my purse. I threw money down onto the table to cover our dinner. I was getting angry. I grabbed my jacket and bag and left without another word.

I hated that it had come to this, but I wasn't going to spend the night somewhere I wasn't wanted. I wish I'd thought about the freezing temperatures before I left the pub with no jacket on. Now I tried to put a scarf, jacket and bag on without dropping anything. Anyone passing would think I was going crazy.

I could feel the tears well up, but I was determined not to cry. After all, I brought this on myself.

"Molly!"

I heard Greg shouting, but I didn't want to stop or turn around. I had one mission and that was to get back to the cottage without slipping on the snow.

"Molly, wait! Please." I could hear his footsteps catching up with me, as his hand grabbed my arm. I just couldn't look him in the eyes. I don't know if I felt ashamed or if I felt stupid.

"Don't go home by yourself." His soft words penetrated my ears, but they meant nothing. Anyone can sound hurt. Anyone can act like they want you around. I'm no stranger to being with a man that doesn't want me.

"I'm not staying when I'm not wanted! Go and enjoy your night! I could do with an early night anyway."

"Where did you get that I don't want you around?"

"You realized that you're going to be with university friends and you don't want to be lumbered with a pregnant woman. I get it. I really do. Just don't..." I pulled my arm out away from his arm and turned to walk away.

"I get that you're pregnant and insecure, but I have never made you feel like that. I have always made it clear to you that I want you in my life."

I stopped dead in my tracks, but kept my back to him. I knew if I turned around, I would crack. "Molly! I want you with me every second of every day! You are the only one who can't see that."

I knew that passersby were watching us. I want the ground to open up and eat me. I think I preferred Greg being quiet, compared to him shouting his feelings in the middle of the street.

"You have a funny way of showing it! What changed? Why the quiet treatment? After the lovely day we had, you had to spoil it!" I threw everything at him and turned to walk back toward him. I felt bad for my part in this mess, but he was no angel either. "I was coming around to the idea that there could be something between us, but there can't be. It isn't fair for us or the kids. If we can't walk away from this for us, then we walk away for the kids."

"There you go again." He shook his head and his eyes were dark and dreamy. I couldn't make proper eye contact. "I wasn't going to do this, but I have to. You really want to know what's wrong with me?"

I finally found courage and looked up at him. I could see the sadness and my heart was breaking inside. "I can't pretend that I don't have feelings for you! I want to be with you every minute of the bloody day! I want to touch you."

His hand came up and rested on my cheek, as the tears rolled from my eyes. I promised myself that I wasn't going to cry, but that was a battle that I was going to lose.

"I want to kiss you every time I look at you." His warm lips rested on mine and I could taste the saltiness of my own tears. "You are the only one who can't see what you mean to me. I said today that I can't force you into my arms, but I'm going to say this..."

His eyes sparkled with unshed tears. I don't know how I have let this get so far. "I can't go on like this anymore. It's killing me watching you go through all of this alone. I want you in my life. I want you both. You're going to tell me that it can't happen because of the baby but that isn't an issue on my part. I want us to have our last night together and if you want me to, then I will walk out of your life. I'll get the guys to finish the work at your farm. You won't have to see me again, apart from being a neighbor."

"What happened to you being in my life any way you could?" I sobbed out each word, making sure I got it all out.

"Look what it's doing to you, Molly. Look what it's doing to us. I can't bear to see you upset, but you won't give us a chance."

"What if I don't want you to walk away?"

"I can't stick around as a friend, Molly. Not after today. This morning when I said that, I was kidding myself. After spending today with you as a couple, I can't go back to a normal tomorrow. I just can't. I won't put you through it anymore. Falling asleep with you in my arms was perfect. Waking up with you in my arms was perfect. Everything about you is perfect."

I rested my hand over his. The outside of his hand was freezing from the cold air. I could only imagine what I looked like standing here.

The silence between us was like a death sentence. I think we were both waiting for the other one to say something else.

"Come with me tonight," he said, as he rubbed his thumb across my cheek.

"I look a mess, Greg."

"You look beautiful, but if you want, we can go get freshened up."

"I would much rather you go by yourself. I can go home and make an early night of it."

"That isn't going to happen. You either come with me or I go home with you." I usually get my way, but he didn't take no for an answer.

"Okay." Greg grew concerned, wondering what option I was going to pick. "I'll come with you, but I'm going back to get freshened up."

"Deal." I was surprised how easily I let him persuade me.

"Ouch!" I quickly moved my hand from Greg's cheek and placed it on my stomach alongside my other hand. I took a couple of deep breaths and suddenly felt the pain ease off as quickly as it came.

"What's wrong, Molly? Is it the baby? Are you okay?" I heard Greg's questions being fired at me a million miles an hour.

"Nothing. Stop worrying. It's just a shooting pain. It's going away." I haven't felt that kind of pain before, but it was gone just as quickly as it appeared.

"Don't tell me not to worry! Maybe we should get you checked out."

"Do you really want to stand here and have another argument?" I barked at him standing my ground this time.

"No, but..."

"But nothing! I'm fine! Let's go get changed before we miss any more of tonight." I was moving away from Greg before we got into another discussion.

I think we both said enough.

***

Now that everything happened the way it did, I feel relieved that we got everything out in the open. I still feel sad, because I have one big decision hanging over my head. We couldn't carry on keeping everything bottled up.

We walked into the big arena sized hall for the gig and the music was pounding through me.

Even though I felt out of place, I put a smile on my face and tried to enjoy our last night together.

I could see that everyone here is young. Maybe Greg and I can be carefree for a couple of hours.

"Molly. What can I get you to drink?" asked Greg, as his big hand on the base of my back, guided me through the crowds.

"Fresh orange and lemonade, if they have it."

I felt naked, the moment his hand left my back to make his way to the crowded bar. Everyone around me was laughing, joking, and having fun. It was time for me to do the same.

Apart from this weekend, I can't remember the last time I did something for myself. Growing up as a teenager and into my early twenties, I would go out with girlfriends to the latest parties followed by clubs. That crazy side fizzled out. I think I only had a crazy couple of years to rebel against my mum and dad fussing about my wellbeing.

Thinking about it now, I wasn't bad. I never did drugs. I didn't drink. I didn't sleep around. I never brought trouble to my parent's door. Which is more than I can say about my brother. He was by far the worst. I lost count how many girls he brought home. My mum was affronted every time he introduced her to a different date, but my dad laughed and gave my brother a pat on the back. I guess it's true when they say that parents treat sons and daughters differently. I felt like they were on my case constantly, whereas Grey was allowed to be reckless.

I just hope that my mum would be proud of the person I have become. I know I'm on the right track, but she would have something to say about me and Greg.

"Sorry about leaving you so long," said Greg, coming back at just the right time.

"Thank you." I accepted my drink and followed his lead. I was hoping that he would lead us to a table.

I could see a rope barrier up ahead with two strapping bouncers guarding the entry but I just kept following Greg.

"Good evening. Can I see your V.I.P. tickets please," said a gruff man, holding his hand out to Greg and me.

I watched Greg fumble in his pocket, so I took the glass from his hand to give him more control. "Thanks Molly."

I didn't know what he was thanking me for, because I was hardly going to let him drop his pint all over the floor. Then we would have no chance moving forward. Greg found the tickets and showed the man.

"Have a good evening," came the gruff voice, with a slight turning up of his lips. I had a funny feeling that was as much of a smile as we were going to get.

"Thank you," said Greg, rescuing his drink from me and taking my hand to walk passed the bouncers.

I don't know if the show of affection was for my benefit or theirs, but I wasn't complaining. After touching him most of the day, I missed having contact with him.

"Greg! My man!" shouted a man in a group of men walking toward us.

Greg's hand let mine go, before I got pulled around from the men's embraces.

The first thing I took notice of, was a couple of men in kilts. I knew then that these were a couple of the guys from Skerryvore.

I stood with a smile, while waiting for their greetings to be finished.

"I didn't think you were going to make it. When ye told me ye were drivin' up yesterday with a friend, I was thrilled at the possibility of catching up with ye," said one of the guys.

I did know the *band*, but I didn't know any of them individually.

Greg turned back to me and held his hand out to me. I suddenly felt self-conscious, so I was glad to take his hand.

"You know I wouldn't miss it for the world, Alex. I came up yesterday afternoon with Molly."

"I thought ye were living the celibate lifestyle in the country." Alex smiled, holding his hand out to shake mine.

"Very funny. Molly? This is Alex. Alex? Molly. Ignore his sense of humor. He thinks he's funny." Joked Greg.

"Nice to meet you, Alex." I extended my hand, but I was taken aback when Alex stepped forward and kissed each of my cheeks.

"Likewise, Molly. Any friend of Greg's is a friend of ours. This is Martin, Daniel, Fraser, and Craig. Sorry, but the other guys are busy just now. I'll introduce you later."

"Hi," I managed to squeak out like a strangled cat, as I lifted my hand to wave to all the faces looking back at me.

"I bet this isn't your idea of fun," said Alex, making me feel very welcome.

"Not at all. I've seen you guys a couple of times in Aberdeen. My brother loves your music."

"We play in Aberdeen quite regularly, but you can make your brother jealous since you're standing here with us...."

"You'll be pleased to know, we have comfy seats in here in if you get tired dancing," said Daniel, pointing over to the seating area.

"Good to know, because I am not a big dancer," I replied.

"You have to dance to our music. Tell her Greg," Daniel said, explaining their rules.

A bell chimed. I had no idea what it was so I looked to Greg for an explanation.

"Right, guys. That's our que. We're on in five," came a voice from a face I didn't know.

"Listen. We'll come and see you when we get a break. Have fun," said Alex, as he high fived Greg.

It suddenly became very quiet, as the band members left us standing in the V.I.P. area. I was now all alone with Greg again.

I was just being stupid.

"Do you fancy taking the weight off your feet?" asked Greg.

"Sure." I followed him to a nearby table very close to the front of the stage. Although I saw the guys perform before, it wasn't up close.

I had a funny feeling that tonight was going to be one to remember.

***

Tonight had been such a great night. I looked at my watch and I was shocked to see that it was 11pm. The gig only had thirty minutes left. Greg pulled me up to the dance floor for all the slow songs.

Hold Me Tonight was the first one. We listened to the lyrics as we danced. Being close to Greg was just beautiful. It was like the words were written for us. *Hold Me Tonight* was exactly what I wanted Greg to do.

His decision of going separate ways once we get home, was back in my mind. All I wanted was tonight to never end.

I didn't want to lose that bond that we had. It was a bond that not many people can achieve in a life time.

I rested my chin on his chest and inhaled his masculine scent. The music stopped but we stayed exactly as we were. I don't think either of us cared what song was coming on next.

On The Road was introduced by the band and my eyes closed, as Greg's arms wrapped around my waist. It felt like we were the only two people in the room.

I couldn't deny that there was chemistry between us, because I've never felt like this before.

He felt like my soulmate.

The music came to a stop and everyone cheered. The band told everyone to get on their feet with their drinks and get their hands in the air.

I pulled back slightly from Greg but left my arms around his neck. I still wasn't ready to break the connection.

"Thank you for the dance," said Greg, very sweetly.

"You're welcome," I said, while smiling.

The crowd was starting to go crazy around us but we were happy to be stuck in between them. The music started beating in my ears and I literally felt my body come alive with the energy.

"You look tired tonight."

"I might be emotionally exhausted but I don't feel tired," I explained, while never once taking my eyes away from his.

"It's my fault. I'm sorry, Molly. I didn't mean to upset you."

"Don't..." I placed a finger over his lips. "Don't spoil what we have now. Let's just enjoy tonight."

I knew we had a lot to talk about but I didn't want to discuss any of it. I just wanted us to be single and unattached. I wanted to be normal for a few hours.

"You do realize that it's nearly midnight. It's almost Sunday. Nearly time to go home."

"We're still here. While we are here in Aviemore, just pretend that there is nothing holding us back." I can't believe that I was saying this and by the looks on Greg's face, he was just as shocked too.

"Kiss me, Greg."

"Molly..."

"Sshh. I want you to kiss me. You're not going to make a pregnant lady beg. Are you?"

I put on my puppy dog eyes and made him laugh. I realized that I dented his pride and he wasn't going to make the first move.

I put my hand back around his neck and played with his hair. I found some courage from somewhere and leaned up against him. I found it hard with my large bump keeping us apart, but I pulled his head down to me and placed my warm, soft lips over his.

At first, our mouths touched and I didn't think that Greg was going to kiss me back.

He pulled back and looked into my eyes. His sparkling brown eyes made my knees weak and I wanted him to kiss me back, but there was nothing.

I went to pull away from him to stop myself from looking desperate, but his hands gripped the fabric of my dress. Again, our eyes met but the passion was screaming from us both.

His hands cupped my face as his lips gently caressed mine. The slow movements made me want more from him. The heat was making me hot as our kiss suddenly became more passionate. His tongue softly entered my mouth as I allowed it. Part of me was glad we were here, because there were still people here. Nothing could happen between us here.

Suddenly we parted from one another and his head rested against my forehead. Both of our breathing was fast and my heart was pounding.

"Do you have any idea what you do to me?" asked Greg, as he caressed my cheeks with his thumbs.

"After that kiss, I have a feeling I know exactly how you feel." I felt like my legs were made of jelly.

"I don't know about you, but I could do with getting out of here to cool off."

I knew exactly what he meant, because I was hot and bothered as well. I have never been attracted to someone as much as I am to him. It was crazy how I was stopping myself from being happy. "Why don't we have a slow walk home?" I suggested.

"If you're not too tired."

"I am perfectly fine," I added, over the music.

"Let's go and say goodbye to the guys. They'll be finished after this song."

I went to move away from Greg, but before I could break our bond, his lips placed a gentle kiss over my wanting mouth.

I had a funny feeling that this was going to be a long emotional night.

***

"You haven't said a word since we left the gig ten minutes ago," said Greg, breaking the silence between us.

I felt like I was on a different planet. I had Greg's hand in mine and I felt like I couldn't stop smiling. I know if I thought about going home, I would be in tears. I took in a deep breath and let the cold air engulf my lungs. I don't know what it is with the air up here, but it made me feel refreshed.

"I think I'm frightened to speak, Greg."

"Why? I'm not that much of an ogre. Am I?" He squeezed my hand, softly.

"If I speak, it means tonight is nearly coming to an end. I'm not ready for it to end, Greg."

"Who said it had to end?"

"We both know that in twelve hours or so, we'll be on our way back to reality. We both know that this can't work in the real world."

"Give me one good reason why it can't work, Mol," he said, pulling us both to a stop and taking my face in his hands. "One good reason and I will take you home and tuck you into bed myself."

His hand rested on my bump and instantly the tears welled up in my eyes. "One reason." His warm lips rested on mine, teasing my senses.

"The kids. We have the kids to think of." My answer was the same every time. It wasn't just two adults in this equation.

"Is that the best you can come up with?"

"Isn't that enough, Greg?"

"Haven't you noticed that my daughter adores you? You are the first woman she has taken to since her mum. I dreaded the first night she met you. I hoped that she would stay in bed, but she is a typical woman. They never do what you want."

I felt Greg's words sink into my heart. *I was a typical woman.* I was doing the opposite of what everyone wanted, but I felt that I was doing the right thing.

Wasn't I?

We both let out a little laugh, as I felt the baby kick Greg's hand. "See? Even this little one is on my side."

"He or she could be just kicking you away from mummy."

"I think it is only the mummy that is doing the kicking."

"Greg..." I placed both of my hands over his hand that was resting on my tummy. "This baby is going to need special care. He or she is going to take up every minute of my time. I don't even know what's going to happen with my business."

My whole life will change when this little baby is born.

"Molly. Have I once made you think that I care about your baby having Down's Syndrome? Have I once pushed you away because your baby is different?"

"No," I sighed.

"Let me help you bring the baby up. We can help one another."

"I can't ask you to bring another man's baby up."

"You didn't ask, you stubborn woman. I offered, because I love you. I want to be the daddy to your baby. You come as a package deal."

"What happens years down the line when you want more from life? You'll hate me for it and I couldn't stand you looking at me with disapproval."

"When did...?"

"Tonight!" I interrupted him from going any further. "You had that look tonight when we were eating dinner. That hurt me more than when Bradley walked out on us."

"I could never reject you or feel disappointed in you, Molly. I was hurting. Do you have any idea what it feels like to love someone so much, but you can't have them?"

"I do."

"You know what I mean then. Give us a chance, Molly."

I heard the pleading in Greg's voice and the sincerity that came with it. I can't help but think that we were saying all of this because we didn't really know what we wanted.

We wanted love. We didn't want to be alone. We wanted family. I just wasn't sure that two ready-made families could be put together and survive.

"Don't go silent on me now, Molly." I have lots to say but I don't know how to say it without being a bitch. "Talk to me, Molly."

"I don't understand why we can't carry on the way we have been?"

"The way we have been?" Greg's raised voice, made me cringe. I know he's frustrated and it's all because of me. I'm scared of commitment. "If you can't see why we can't carry on like this, then you're not as smart as I thought you were."

"Don't you dare patronize me, Greg! I can't give you what you want! It will never work, so stop forcing me to make decisions!"

I was the one doing the shouting now, but I was angry.

"You can give me everything I want and more." His quiet words, echoed in my ears as his hand wiped away a stray tear. "You're choosing this, Molly. It's not that you can't be with me, you won't allow yourself to be with me."

I felt the sobs catch at the back of my throat, as Greg's words hit home. "We could be good together. We could be a family. Me, you, and the kids."

Greg's lips placed a kiss on my forehead, as I felt him slip through my fingers. "I'm done, Molly. I'm going to grab a pint at the pub. I'll give you time to go to bed and find your own space. We'll leave at one o'clock tomorrow." His body quickly turned to walk away and I immediately felt empty without him beside me.

"Greg!" I shouted a little louder than I wanted, but it made him turn around and look at me. "I'm sorry for leading you on."

"Sorry? I should have seen it coming. My mum told me as a boy to watch out for the quiet ones. I guess she was right."

"I do love you, Greg."

"Clearly, not enough." His words stung me like a bee.

"I just want you to know that I meant every touch...every kiss."

"I don't understand you at times, Mol. How can you push me away and then say that?"

"I'm not ready for commitment. Maybe when I am, we can give us a try." I didn't want him to walk away from me like this.

"I can't wait forever, Molly. Concentrate on you and the baby and I will respect your wishes and leave you alone."

"Greg..." I stepped one foot closer but he held his hands up to stop me going any closer. I felt the knife penetrate my heart.

I guess it's exactly what I deserve. It's what I did to him for weeks. "Go back to the cottage, Molly. It's just across the road."

"I know where it is, but I don't want to leave things like this between us."

"There is no us. You've made that perfectly clear." Every one of my emotions floated to the surface and I did the only thing I could do. I turned to cross the road.

I needed to get off the street before people saw this heavily pregnant, blubbering mess.

I was aware of the thick snow turning to ice, but I tried my hardest to get home in one piece. I was a mess, but it was all my own fault. I did this to myself and now I had to deal with the consequences.

I want to scream, shout, and punch anything in the vicinity. I probably just made the worst mistake of my life. It's becoming the story of my life.

I fumbled in my bag through blurry eye's, to get the keys out for the cottage. I wanted to get inside and just fall asleep. I hoped to wake up in the morning and realize that this was one big nightmare.

The moment I got inside the cottage, I switched the lamp on and threw my bag down on the couch. The glimmer of light was still coming from the open coal fire. The cottage was so warm and cozy, but here I was on my own. Again.

I walked through to the kitchen and poured myself a glass of milk. I'm not a big fan of milk, but I had a weird craving for it.

"You're very lively tonight, little one. Some of your kicks are hurting mummy." My hand rubbed circles on my tummy as I drank some of my milk. "Are you trying to tell me that you're disappointed in me, too?"

This was one of those moments that I wanted the answers to jump out at me, but I wasn't so lucky.

Suddenly, this intense pain shot through my tummy. Through the sheer panic, my glass of milk went crashing to the floor. The shooting pain had me now crouched down onto my knees.

Fear struck me again. It was too soon for the baby to come. I was too far from a hospital. I was on my own.

All the negative thoughts entered my mind and fear kept me paralyzed. What the hell was I going to do?

I tried to crawl to get my bag from the living room, but the pain made me stop to breathe it out.

I knew I needed to get help and anyone would do right now, as long as they could help me get to a hospital.

I managed to get to my bag, but to my horror, my phone was dead. I shouted out of pure frustration. This was just my luck to go into labor in the middle of nowhere.

There was no way that I was going to make it to my room to get the charger. I struggled to get a few feet from the kitchen and the pain was getting stronger each time it hit me.

I had no idea what I was supposed to be doing. "Greg!" I yelled, as I thought I had a contraction. I know I was wasting my breath, because Greg wouldn't hear me.

That man loves you, you stupid cow.

I had a mission to get to my charger, so I could call Greg but I couldn't even get out to the hall. I knew I was exhausting myself and I needed to calm down.

Just when I thought I was on my own I heard the front door click open. I immediately felt relief as hope washed through me. "Greg!" I yelled with panic.

"Molly. What's wrong?" He crouched down in front of me, moving my hair away from face.

"I think the baby is on its way," I sobbed.

"It's too soon! Isn't it?"

"I know it is. I can't lose him, Greg!" Just seeing Greg's worried expression, made me realize how serious this could be.

"I'm going to help you get up onto the couch and I'll phone an ambulance. Don't worry, sweetheart. You're going to be fine."

"Stop being nice to me! I don't deserve it! I'm a complete bitch!" I could feel my heart breaking.

"Forget about it. The main thing now is you and the baby." Greg's strong arms helped me to my feet. "That's a girl. Keep breathing, honey."

"I can't sit down! Please make it stop!" I rested my head on Greg's chest, as I breathed out through another contraction.

"Shit!" Greg continued to rub my back.

"What? What is it?" I asked.

"My phone must be in the pub." I let out a yell as my tummy contracted harder this time. "Molly, listen to me." I looked up but grabbed a hold of Greg's jacket for support. "I'm going to run across to the pub to get help. I will be two minutes, if that."

"No! You can't leave me!" The panic hit me again and I tightened my grip on his jacket.

"I need to get help! Lean on the breakfast bar and keep breathing. I promise I'll be back in under two minutes."

I let him guide me over to the breakfast bar, as we stepped over the broken glass and splattered milk. "You've had a smashing time," Greg joked.

"I'm sorry about the mess. I'll clean it up."

"I don't care about the mess, Molly. My main concern is you and this little one. Now hold on and I will be back."

"Promise?"

"I promise." Greg went to leave me but I pulled his jacket back to stop him.

"I know I have no right to ask you this after tonight, but I can't deliver this baby on my own!" I let out another pained shriek.

"Breath through it, doll. That's it. You're doing great."

"I don't feel great!" I snapped back, as my head rested on my arm on the breakfast bar.

"You won't be doing this alone. Once I come back, I won't leave your side until this little one is here."

"What if he doesn't...?"

"Enough! He's going to be fine." Greg rushed off to get help.

He is being so calm. How can he be calm when I'm here flapping like a chicken? He's doing everything right to get the baby and me to a hospital and I am petrified that something is going to happen to my baby.

The midwife told me to get to a hospital as soon as possible when I went into labor, so they could monitor the baby's heartbeat. Here I am with no technology to monitor him, no nurse, and no doctor. Everything was going wrong. I even forgot to tell Greg to just use my phone with the charger.

"Molly! I'm back!" shouted Greg, as he came back in and took his jacket off. "The landlord of the pub is phoning the ambulance and the landlady went to get the resident GP. I told them about the baby having Down's Syndrome, so we are all set.

"It's too soon, Greg."

"Everything is going to be fine. It's only a few weeks before your due date, so don't worry too much. Walk with me to the couch."

"I can't sit down, Greg!" I was trying to relax but another pain hit me twice as hard and then I would panic again.

"Why don't we get you on to the bed, then?"

"My baby can't be born here!"

"You might have to if the ambulance doesn't get here in time."

"Please, make it stop!" I wasn't ready for this. I wasn't prepared to bring my baby into the world.

"Give me your hands and walk with me. I won't let you fall. I've got you."

I trusted Greg with my life. I gave him my hands and let him guide me to the bedroom. Just as we made it into the room, I heard someone come into the cottage.

"We're in here!" he shouted.

I was so embarrassed to be seen like this but I hoped it was the doctor. It might put my nerves at rest.

"I'm Dr. Livingstone and this is Linda. Can you tell me your name?" Good. A female doctor.

"Molly," both Greg and I stated at the same time.

"Okay, Molly. I'm going to help you until the paramedics get here. I don't want to scare you, but the road is blocked. The fire crew is trying to clear a tree from an accident. They will be here as quickly as they can."

"No! I need a hospital now! My baby needs special care!"

"I trained in midwifery. I will look after you."

"No! My baby has Down's Syndrome," I yelled.

"I know. Linda told me on the way over here. I have oxygen here with me and plenty of supplies. I need you to calm down, because that isn't helping you or the baby."

"Please, look after my baby!" I felt tears fall from my eyes, because I couldn't hold them back anymore.

"You have my word. Now, before you lie down, can I get you to slip your tights and pants off? Then we'll get you into bed and as comfortable as possible. Can you help your partner while I get set up here?

"Oh...I'll wait outside until she's set," muttered Greg.

"Step to it! Your partner needs your support!" snapped the doctor.

I let out a scream, as my water broke and soaked the floor. I burst into tears with embarrassment. "I'm sorry, Greg."

"Stop apologizing, darling. Let's get you sorted and into bed."

"You don't have to help me," I sobbed.

"I want to help you. That's if you don't mind me helping to get your clothes off."

"Don't leave me. Please don't leave me."

I know many women go through childbirth, but I never realized what it's like. I've heard so many people say that you leave your pride at the door when you go into labor, but now I know exactly what they mean.

I know I'm crazy. I can't commit to Greg, but I can allow him to help me give birth to my baby.

"Linda! Can you get us towels and hot water please? It seems like this baby is in a hurry to meet mum and dad," said the doctor, calmly.

I heard exactly what she said, so must have Greg, but neither one of us corrected her.

No matter what happens now, things are going to be different between me and Greg.

GREG

"Molly. The doctor knows what she's doing, so please calm down." It's easier for me, because it isn't me giving birth.

Helping Molly get onto the bed was hard, because she was struggling. I just wanted to take it all away from her.

"Make it stop!" yelled Molly, squeezing my hand until it was ready to snap off.

"You're doing great, Mol."

I hope I never have to see the prick who walked out on Molly. I don't know how any man can get a woman pregnant and then just bail on them.

I'm pissed off, because I would do anything to be with Molly. Thanks to some idiot, her confidence has been shaken.

I will do anything for this woman and I never thought I would say that again.

"Is this normal for her to be in so much pain?" I was trying to stay calm for Molly's sake, but I was getting stressed.

I have Kayleigh, but I never got to see her birth. I have no idea if this is normal or not.

"It's all perfectly normal," said the doctor.

She looks at me, hoping I'll stop asking silly questions, but she kept concentrating on her watch. "Your contractions are close together, Molly. You shouldn't have too much longer to go."

I want to do something, but all I can do is sit beside Molly and let her squeeze my hand.

I really feel helpless.

"See? Not long before you get to meet your son or daughter," I said moving the hair away from Molly's face.

It was meaningless things I was doing to make her comfortable, but I didn't want to make things worse.

I'm glad this isn't an everyday occurrence, because I can't cope. I don't know how doctors and midwifes go through this daily.

How did tonight turn out like this?

Molly

"Okay, Molly. Now that we have you comfortable, I can check to see what stage of labor you're at. Greg? Do you want to sit behind Molly, just to give her support? She looks exhausted."

"Eh...sure." Poor Greg didn't know what to do or say, but he followed the doctor's orders.

I wish this happened hours ago when we were so close. I felt awkward now, so I can only imagine how he must feel.

"Good news Molly! You're fully dilated. When you feel ready to start pushing this baby out, we're here with you," explained the doctor.

"It's too soon!" I cried, resting my head back onto Greg's shoulder. "You have to stop this from happening!"

"Molly. Listen to me." I looked up at the doctor and I felt like my whole world was spinning around me. "This baby is coming now. You need to push."

"I can't!" I yelled back at the doctor with as much power as I could.

"Molly. Sweetheart." Greg pulled my chin around to him, so I could focus on him. "You can do this. Stop with the *can't*, because it's getting boring," We both laughed together while everything stopped around us. "I am going to do this with you."

Only me and Greg understood what he was talking about, so the look of confusion on the doctor's face was rather quite amusing.

"I need to push! Another one is coming!"

"Good! Molly, when a contraction like this comes, you just push with everything you have."

This contraction was different. It was stronger, but I felt in control for the first time tonight. "Good! That wasn't too bad. Was it?" asked the doctor.

"Not too bad for you! I don't see you lying here trying to push this baby out!" I really wanted to be nippy to her. "Another one is coming!"

"Good. Just do the same thing." The doctor held my knees in place.

"You're doing great! Keep going," Greg whispered in my ear, as I squeezed the life from his poor hands.

"I can see the baby's head, Molly. One more push and you will meet your baby."

I was exhausted. I was glad that Greg's body was keeping me upright, because I don't think I would have the energy on my own. "Greg. I'm sorry about tonight."

"Molly, just forget it. We have the rest of our lives to sort out our problems. Just push out this little bundle of joy."

Just push. I hoped and prayed this was the final push, because I needed the baby out. I needed to know my child was okay.

The pain was unlike anything I have ever felt. The moment my baby was born I forgot all about it and concentrated on what was happening now. "Is he or she okay? Is my baby breathing?"

"You have a little boy, Molly," said the doctor.

"He isn't crying!" The fear washed through me again as Greg wrapped his arms around my shoulders and placed soft kisses on my head. "What's wrong with him?"

"It was a quick delivery and he didn't get a chance to get all the mucus out. This will help him."

I watched the doctor suck stuff from his mouth with something that looked like a syringe. The tears ran down my face, as we waited anxiously to hear him cry and see him take a breath. "I can't lose him, Greg."

"You won't lose him. He's a fighter, just like his mummy."

Suddenly this high-pitched squawk echoed through the room and we all breathed a sigh of relief. Now I was crying tears of joy.

I felt my body relax back in to Greg's embrace as I watched the doctor check my son over.

I was disturbed when Greg went to move away from behind me, so I caught his hand to stop him. "Please stay." I pleaded with him.

I could see him thinking about it, but when he sat back down behind me, I was happy and content in his arms.

"Would you like to meet your son?" asked the doctor as she offered me my baby wrapped in a towel.

Of course, I accepted him with open arms. His little body fit perfectly in my arms. I couldn't believe that it was all over with.

He was perfect.

***

Just a few short hours after giving birth and I was safely in the hospital getting checked over. The pediatrician came for my baby the moment I arrived in hospital, because the paramedics had radioed over and told them everything that happened.

I feel lost without my bundle of joy in my arms. I cradled him in my arms from the moment he made his first cry and now I just want him back with me.

Greg was calling my dad and Sylvia to let them know what happened. He also needed to call his mum to let her know that we would be running a little bit late.

I was glad to see Greg peek his head around the corner. His smile lit up the room. "Are you okay for visitors?"

"Are you kidding?" I asked. "I think you're more than a visitor."

"Your dad wanted to come up here but I told him to hang tight until we know what's happening."

"Thank you." I breathed a sigh of a relief, because I couldn't be doing with everyone fussing over me.

"You look exhausted, Molly. Maybe I should leave and let you get some rest."

"I would really like you to stay, but I'll understand if you need to get home to pick up Kayleigh."

"I don't need to go anywhere. My mum knows that I'm staying with you. I just meant that I could go back to the cottage until you rest."

"Why?"

"Why, what?" asked Greg, sitting on the side of my bed.

"Why are you staying with me? I've been cruel. I don't deserve you being here for me."

"Yeah. You've been a mean..." He smiled taking my hand in his. "I'm going to say this one last time, Molly. I love you. I want to be with you and your perfect little boy. I want you both in my life forever."

The tears welled up in my eyes and I felt my throat get dry, as I tried to think about what I was going to say. "Greg. Not many men would have done what you did tonight. I will never be able to thank you enough, for being there for us when we needed you most. I do love you, Greg Macintosh. I'm sorry it has taken me so long to see things clearly."

Greg's mouth claimed mine stopping me from talking a lot of nonsense. The minute our mouths become one the love was evident between us.

When the door opened, a doctor and midwife pushed my son into the room. His tiny cot was placed by my bedside and the midwife handed him to me, carefully. "Do you have a name for him?" she asked.

"What do you think about, Kian?" I asked Greg, as he rubbed his thumb over the baby's cheek.

"I think it's perfect. Just like his mummy."

I have never in my life felt so happy and in love. I've dreamt of this moment for as long as I can remember. My hopes of a family disintegrated when my ex left me pregnant. Here I am now with my perfect moment.

*Ou*r perfect moment.

Chapter 12

New Beginnings

Molly

48 hours after giving birth and we are on way home. Kian was a couple of weeks early but he has been given a clean bill of health apart from his Down's Syndrome.

We had a fresh start ahead of us. We are ready to face whatever life throws at us.

Greg has spent the last 48 hours making sure we had everything we needed. Although Kian isn't his, he has accepted him. I can't believe that I thought he would treat him differently. The bond that they are going to have is unbelievable.

"Are you sure that you're ready to face everyone? People will be stopping by at some point to see how you both are," said Greg, looking through his mirror to see my reaction in the backseat.

"I'm still getting used to everything. I'm not sure that I'm ready to start answering questions." I know that I probably sound selfish, but I need time to take everything in.

"Are you feeling okay, Molly?"

"Yeah." Everything was going to be too much for me, but I can't quite put my finger on why I was feeling so anxious.

"You've been very quiet," Greg added.

I spotted the Stirling sign as we came off the motorway and I felt like my heart was going to jump out of my chest. We were ten minutes away from home. "In Aviemore, it was just us but now we're going home. I'm terrified of being alone. What if something happens?"

"First of all, you're not going to be alone, because you have Sylvia and your family. You have me." Our eyes locked together through the mirror and I couldn't stop myself from smiling. "Nothing is going to happen. You have both been given a clean bill of health."

"You know what I mean Greg. He isn't like a normal child."

"If you keep thinking like this then you're going to drive yourself crazy."

"I know you're right, but I can't help it. It's all I can think about." I took in a deep breath and held it for a few seconds.

"Maybe when the midwife comes to check on you and Kian, you should tell her how you're feeling."

"I am not crazy, Greg!" I snapped, but didn't mean to.

"I never said you were. You could have Postpartum Depression. You could just be tired. It could be a number of normal things that happen after a woman gives birth."

Reality suddenly hit me. Maybe he was right. Maybe a good sleep in my own bed would do me the world of good.

Maybe, maybe, maybe. I had to try to take control over my life again.

***

Pulling up in my driveway, I saw that there was no one around. I was very pleased. It would give me time to settle down in my own surroundings and get used to being a mum.

I left here on Friday, thinking that I still had a couple of weeks left. Yet, here I am returning from our long weekend away with a tiny baby to look after.

"Well little man. This is your new home," I said, running my finger across his soft little cheek.

Greg opened the back door and took off the seat belt. He made me look him in the eyes. The goosebumps appeared with any contact I had with Greg. "Don't think about pushing me away now that we're home. I meant every word I said. I'm in this for the long haul, Molly."

"I'm so glad to hear that, because I'm not ready to let you go." I smiled and took in every inch of Greg's beautiful face.

His warm lips met mine and our tongues intertwined, as we shared our first intimate moment back home. "Let's get this little one into a nice warm house."

I'm glad he broke our kiss and thought about Kian, because his kiss melted any brain cells I had left. He lifts the car seat out and waits for me to join them. I only felt whole when I was touching Greg in some way.

I want this to be our new beginning. I want to see where we go from here, because we have so much to sort out. But right now my little hand in his felt secure as we took the small walk into my own house.

The heat hit us the moment we step over the threshold. "Sylvia has been here to put the fire on," I explain, as Greg walks off into my living room with Kian.

Gizmo jumps to me from his basket in the kitchen and I can't stop myself from bending down to kiss and cuddle him.

"Coffee!" I shouted to Greg, as I turn the kettle on with Gizmo in my arms.

"Molly. You better come here a moment." Curiosity got the better of me and I threw my bag down on the table and let Gizmo go.

"What's wrong?"

"Surprise!" I turn the corner into the living room and my family and friends are there. Greg's family is there, as well.

I am shocked, to say the least. Greg placed Kian's car chair down on the floor and walks back to.

"I had no idea. I would have stopped them if I knew."

"I can do without this today," I whisper as he stood in front of me.

"One hour and I will get them all out."

"Molly!" yelled Greg's daughter, running up to give me a cuddle.

"Careful sweetheart. Molly is still a little sore," explained Greg, to his very excited 6 year old.

"She's okay," I responded. "Hiya sweetie. How have you been for gran and grandad?"

"What did you call the baby? Can I see him?" I laughed, because I wasn't getting an answer to my questions. She was too excited to see Kian and I can't blame her.

"Of course you can see him. His name is Kian." I looked over at everyone fussing over Kian, as he laid content and sleeping. Kayleigh managed to push her way in to kneel in front of Kian's chair. I'm glad to see that her determination got her up close to the little man. After all they would need to get used to one another.

I take in a deep breath and let it go with a sigh of relief. Everyone was leaving me alone, but I knew that wouldn't last.

"Molly," said my dad, coming up to embrace me in a big bear hug. He squeezed the life from me. “You did a grand job bringing that little man into the world. Come and get a drink to celebrate."

"I’m good. Thank you, dad. I’m going to get some coffee." I made my quick exit out of the living room and I leaned over my breakfast bar and rested my head into my hands. I wanted the ground to open up and swallow me whole.

I just wanted a day on my own with Greg and the kids.

Greg

"Is she okay, Greg? My little girl seems rather distant today," Molly's dad asked, as we both watch her leave the living room.

"She’s exhausted, sir. What was meant to be a relaxing weekend, ended in her giving birth and being stranded in the cottage." Just thinking about our ordeal, sent shivers down my spine.

"I thought you were in the hospital when you called."

"We were, but only after the birth. A resident doctor helped Molly deliver Kian. It was a scary time for everyone. We didn't know what was going to happen, but this little man came out fighting."

"She must have been so scared."

"She was, sir. We both were terrified for a little while. I didn't think to tell you to hold off with the celebration." I tried to be diplomatic and tell them in a polite way that Molly didn't want them all here.

"It will do Molly good to know that her family and friends are here for her."

If only he knew how wrong he was. I was worried about Molly's state of mind, but I would keep that to myself for the time being.

I couldn't stop smiling, as I watched everyone fussing over Kian, while he slept peacefully. I was torn between staying in here with the baby and going off to see Molly. However, my mum's arms around my waist took my attention back to the here and now.

"I'm confused darling," I looked at my mum curiously and waited for her to elaborate. "I haven't seen you smile like that for a long time, but you look like you have the weight of the world on your shoulders."

"I'm happy mum. Very happy."

"I can see that, but what's going on with that beautiful girl?" I look around my mum to look at my daughter fussing with Kian. "Not your daughter. Molly. Is she okay?"

I knew if anyone was going to see it, it would be my mum. She has a big heart and will see if anyone is hurting in anyway. "I'm not sure, mum. She was quiet all the way home."

I shrugged my shoulders and took a deep breath in. I knew I could trust my mum for advice. "She said a few things since the baby was born, like she thinks something is going to happen to the baby. She's going to drive herself crazy."

"It's only normal, son. Kian is a special baby and Molly is bound to worry about him. I watched you while you slept in your crib for weeks after you were born."

"I'm worrying for nothing?"

"About the motherly instinct, yes Greg. I'm more concerned that she couldn't get out of here fast enough."

"I don't know what to do for the best, mum. I love her to pieces, but I hate to see her hurting over something we have no control over."

"Let me talk to her." I shook my head, but my mum's hand on my arm stopped me in my tracks. "I won't say a word of what you've told me."

"Okay, but be gentle with her."

"Can you imagine me being any other way?" asked my mum, before she walked away.

I carefully scanned the large room and took in all the happy faces. It's amazing how happy a new baby can make people feel. Kian isn't mine but I feel a strong connection to the little lad and will do everything in my power to give him everything he needs. I can provide the love and affection he will need throughout his life. I can provide all the essentials too. I can be a father figure to him.

It's just a pity that life isn't as straight forward.

Molly

Pouring the hot water into my coffee, was like something awakening me from my dreams. The smell of the coffee hit my nose and I finally realized that I was in my kitchen, when I really should be in the living room with my baby boy.

I missed coffee so much while I was pregnant. I stopped drinking it the moment I found out I was pregnant and now I can't get enough of it to boost my energy.

"Hi Molly, sweetheart. How are you feeling?" said Greg's mum, as she sat down at the kitchen table.

"Coffee?" I asked, before I made my mind up what to do.

"I've just had one."

I've been waiting for someone like her to ask me that most important question. If it had been anyone else, I would have probably either bit their head off or told them what they wanted to hear.

"Apart from being overwhelmed and tired, I'm okay." I took my cup from the worktop and made my way over to sit down at the table with Greg's mum. I felt like I needed to give her five minutes of my time, before I rescued my son from everyone else.

"I can remember when I had Greg. I laid awake for weeks and just watched him sleep. Sleep deprivation must have taken me every night. I would wake up every morning and panic that he wouldn't be okay. Then when I bounced out of the bed, I saw two big bright blue eye's staring back at me."

"Why are you telling me this?" I didn't mean to sound ungrateful, so I tried to keep a smile on my face.

" I could see that same look in your eyes when you walked through the door."

"Does it ever go away?" I asked.

"Mothers instincts never go away, but you learn to realize that you're wasting precious moments when you worry to that extent."

"Greg mentioned Postpartum Depression earlier. Do you think he's right?"

"I know Greg loves you very much, sweetheart. Give yourself a couple of weeks to adjust to motherhood and if you still feel down and under pressure, then you will know to get help. Right now, I think it could just be pregnancy blues. We all get them."

"I hope you're right."

"I'm here if you need anything. I have a new grandson that I would love to get to know, so if you need anything at all, you just pick up the phone and call. I know he isn't mine by blood, but that won't make a blind bit of difference to us."

I got up slowly and took Greg's mum into my arms. I felt a hundred times better just having a quick conversation with another woman. Knowing that she wants to treat Kian like Kayleigh, has made my heart swell.

After my little meltdown, I feel a lot happier. I touched Greg's arm slightly as I passed him in the living room. I'm sure he was stuck on that spot, because he hasn't moved since we came in.

I placed my cup down on the coffee table and squeezed through everyone to get to my baby. I'm surprised he is still sleeping with everyone making so much noise around him.

I bent down carefully to unstrap him from his chair. His tiny body fit perfectly into my arms, as I cradled him to my chest. I held my hand out for Kayleigh and I left everyone standing, as I sat down on the couch.

If Greg and I were going to make this work, then I needed to bond with Kian and Kayleigh. I needed to include her in everything, so she didn't feel left out.

I spotted Greg standing with my brother Gray, staring through me with a ridiculous grin on his face.

Out of us both, he was the one who knew we would work.

His smug look is only shouting I told you so.

Chapter 13

3 Months Later

Molly

Three months passed by so quickly. I settled into motherhood nicely and I was loving every minute of it. I was glad it was just a touch of the pregnancy blues, because I would have hated to have anything more serious. I know many women go through it, but I have enough going on without adding something else into the mix.

Kian has become one happy, spoiled little boy. He has us all wrapped around his little fingers. He just has to make a noise and Greg is fussing over him. If he drops anything, then Kayleigh runs and picks it up for him. He is never going to need to learn anything as long as he has those two doing everything for him.

I was surprised how much Greg's family has accepted me and Kian into their lives. I expected to be left on the sidelines, until Greg and I had been together for a while. Both Greg's mum and dad welcomed us with open arms.

My family, on the other hand, shocked the life out of me. Apart from when Kian was first born, I haven't seen them. I keep trying to put my crazy doubts to the back of my head but I can't help but think it's because Kian has Down's Syndrome. I know it's crazy, because family should stick around no matter.

We are now into March and Greg and his team have worked day and night to get my barn converted.

Every day this week, I wrapped Kian up, put him into his pram, and bring him out to the barn. My office is now complete. In April, I will be ready to accept new clients.

This is me on the road to success. I know it's going to take a long time for me to make it a successful business, but I will put every spare minute into my work. This is the only way to make a future for my children.

"Molly!" Greg shouted.

He knew where to find me, so I think he just shouts so he doesn't scare me. "Have you lost someone?" asked Greg, as I hear him approach my office.

I have no idea what he was talking about. "Not that I know of."

"Gizmo," he said, as he entered my office. “He was along the farm road. I picked him up and drove him back."

"That little shit! He’s getting too good at wandering and it really isn't like him." I was annoyed at my little pug, because he never moved from my side until we moved out here. He must think the more room he has, the more he can explore.

"He’s exploring," said Greg, laughing at him.

"He won't be exploring when I get my hands on him," I joked, as Greg crossed my office floor to wrap me in his arms.

"How are my favorite people doing?" His warm lips caressed mine, as he teased my every sense.

"We’re all the better for seeing you."

"Stealing my lines now?"

"Would I do a thing like that?" I smiled, taking him all in.

"Eh...yeah," We both laughed. I felt secure when I was in his arms. "I’m glad I caught you alone, because I have something to run passed you."

"Why do I get the feeling that I’m not going to like this?" I asked out of curiosity.

"Don't be silly, Molly. You can tell me to mind my own business. I did this for the opening of my own business and it really helped kick start things."

"I’m all ears." I sat up on my desk and waited to hear what Greg had to say. I could use all the help I could get.

"I know you want to open up next month, but for any new business it's difficult. What about throwing a grand opening party? You invite all the local businesses and local residents to see what you have to offer. You have incentives for new clients. I still say that is what got me off the ground."

I sat still, taking everything in carefully. It was a fabulous idea. I don't know why I never thought of it. I could see my grand opening party in full swing.

"That's a wonderful idea. I can pick a date toward the end of April." Then I slumped down on the desk as reality hit me.

"What is it?" he asked.

"It's a fabulous idea. It would be successful, but are you forgetting that Kian's here?"

" I'm not forgetting about my buddy, but I don't understand why that matters."

"Because he takes up all my time. A party will take time and effort. Something I don't have right now."

"Molly. When are you going to realize that you're not alone? I'm here for you both. I'll help you with the party and help you with Kian."

"You already do enough."

"If I didn't want to do it, then I wouldn't. It works both ways, because you help me with my life. My Daughter. My family. We're a team now and a pretty good one, at that."

No one ever supported me like Greg has and I feel emotional just listening to him. "So what do you say, Molly?"

"I say let's do it." I lean into Greg and let him take my mouth with his. His big hands get tangled in my hair, as our bodies reacted to the chemistry between us.

Neither one of us care that we're in my office where any one can walk in. I think the lack of passion between us at the beginning has been simmering away on the back heat. My fingers fumble with Greg's buttons on his cardigan, just as Kian starts to cry.

We both sigh. It's like everything waits until Greg and I are together. If it isn't Kian, it's something else. "I love that little man to pieces but I need to have a man to man chat with him."

I laugh, as I hop down from my desk to attend to my son. "He's telling you to keep your hands off of his mummy." I joked, winking over at Greg playfully as he sat down in the chair.

"Don't worry. By the time I have a word with him he will be on my side."

"Don't bet on it Buster. This little one knows where his bread is buttered."

Cooing over my son and joking with Greg, is the best feeling in the world. It's crazy thinking back to the beginning when I was willing to push Greg away. I can't imagine my life without him now.

To think how far we have come in such a short time is absolutely crazy. We've achieved so much.

Some days, I still have slight doubts about our relationship but it's not because of anything we have done or said. What frightens me more, is losing the one person I can call my friend, my lover, and my soulmate.

Chapter 14

Opening Day

Molly

The last four weeks were spent getting things ready for my grand opening.

With a new baby, things have been hectic, but with the help of Greg and Sylvia, everything has been so much smoother.

I was nervous that my family is coming down from Aberdeen to support me. It's the first time they have been back since I arrived home with my new baby. It’s crazy, because in those four months, my life has changed dramatically. I am not the same person that I was a year ago.

I’m settled here in my new life and no one ever thought I would say that. They would have put money on my return when I had the baby. I knew I had to prove everyone wrong and live my life the way I wanted to.

I can see how wrong everyone was. I felt like everyone judged me, but I had a bigger story to tell here.

"Molly!" I heard Greg shouting for me, as I sat at my desk in my pajamas with my hair in rollers, trying to pass some time.

"I’m in my office!" I shouted back. I had no idea where he was coming from.

"I should have guessed when the pram was gone. I thought you would like to know that your family has just arrived."

I immediately felt my mood deflate.

I love my family with all my heart, but I feel let down by them at the moment. Their support has been poor since I moved away and had Kian. I feel hurt.

"Molly." Greg sat on my desk and turned my chin so I could look him in the eye. "You can tell me to mind my own business if you like, but I know something is bothering you."

"I’m fine, Greg."

"If that's all you want to tell me then okay, but I know you better than that." He started to walk away.

"I'm just worried about today. I want it to work, but something is telling me to look out for disaster."

Greg's full frame crouched down in front of me and took my face in his hands. His warm eyes made me relax slightly as the goosebumps spread over me. "Today is going to be perfect. You put so much hard work into this grand opening and nothing is going to go wrong. I just tacked the fairy lights to the barn, so everything is done. Even if you show up in rollers and pjs, you will still look fabulous."

"I don't deserve you," I stated, as I placed my hand over Greg's.

"I think you will find it's me who doesn't deserve you. Are we going to get ready to greet your guests?"

His warm lips touched mine and as usual the fireworks exploded inside of me. I could have quite easily stayed here all day with Greg, but his cold hands led me to my son before we headed back to the house to see my family.

***

Walking through my newly renovated house was so peaceful. I looked around for any signs of life but everyone must have made their way out to the barns.

I stop in front of the mirror in my hall and take a few deep breaths. I've waited for this moment for so long, but now that it's here I'm a bag of nerves.

I need to get out of this house before I run in the opposite direction, so I step out of my front door and let the fresh country air hit me.

This is home.

I make my way through all the cars that have accumulated in my drive. I stop suddenly and feel that weird feeling that someone is watching me. I look around to make sure nothing is wrong. Then I shake my head and breathe in a sigh of relief.

"Molly," came a voice that made me jump. "Are you okay?" asked Greg, as he rubbed his hands up and down my arms.

"I’m better now that you’re here."

"You look like you saw a ghost."

"Nerves are getting the better of me." I hope that it will be enough of an explanation.

"When you walk through those doors and see how busy it is, your nerves will vanish." Greg's hand outstretched to me and of course, I accept any part of him. I know with him by myside, I will get through anything.

Greg lets my hand go before we enter my barn. I’m confused, so I stop and turn back toward him. "Are you coming?"

"I wouldn't miss it for the world, but this is your day. You need to get to know people for yourself and not through me. I'll only be a few feet away from you at all times, but I want you to enjoy your day. You deserve this."

"Kian..."

"Me or Sylvia will always be with him, so don't worry." I take a deep breath in and let it go. I'm trying to gain courage before this event even starts.

"Before I go in here, I just want to tell you how much I love you. The way you treat Kian like he's your own, just touches my heart in a way I didn't know was possible."

"I love you and that little man. I can't imagine life without you both. We're happy together. We are complete."

"Let's get this show on the road." I pushed up onto my toes to reach Greg's lips with my own. This was the Dutch courage that I needed in order to face everyone.

As I turn the barn door, I took a glass of Champagne from the waitress greeting everyone as they entered. The whole room broke into cheers as I walked through the crowds of people congratulating me. I feel like royalty laughing and smiling with all my new prospective clients.

"Hi Molly. I'm Christopher from Butler's Farm." He looked and sounded like a typical farmer.

"Hi, Christopher. You need to excuse me for being rude, because I'm not great with the area yet."

"That's understandable. I'm just outside of Airth and a stone's throw away from Airth Castle. You should get yourself one of those Nat Sav things, which will keep you right until you get your bearings." I couldn't help but laugh when it dawned on me that Christopher meant a Sat Nav.

"Great minds think alike, because Greg fitted a new *Sat Nav* to my car the other day. I think he was fed up with giving me directions to get home." We laughed and it felt good.

"Ah, young Greg." Christopher's laugh had me curious. "I can remember when he was your son's age. We all knew that he would do well for himself. You've got a good one there, hen. I'm glad that he found someone like you after what happened with his daughter's mother."

"We both had a tough ride, Christopher, but together we feel complete." I can't believe that I am sharing my feelings with a stranger, but I want to shout it from the rooftop.

"I can see that, my dear. Hold onto one another now. I have taken up enough of your time today. Just point me in the direction of where to sign up and I'll leave you to mingle."

"It's been lovely meeting you, Christopher. Once you have done the tour, my office is at the other end with all the paperwork set up. I'll be in touch next week to come and see you."

"I look forward to it," said Christopher, as he shuffled away to do the tour.

One thing I learned about farmers is how loyal they are to their lifestyle. I haven't come across one nasty person in this area, yet. Everyone is friendly and welcoming. I half expected to be treated as the outsider until they got to know me, but I have been treated like royalty by each person that lives in a 10 -mile radius.

I look around to see that I'm on my own. Everyone is laughing and enjoying themselves. I can't ask for any more than that.

My nerves were for nothing this morning.

"Can I have everyone's attention please?" I turn slowly to the stage to see Greg getting everyone's attention.

I had no idea that this was going to happen, so all I can do is smile. "First of all, I apologize for butting in today! I have been thinking of the perfect time to do this and today has worked out beautifully! I'm so proud of how far Molly has come over the last few months! She moved this place into the 21st century! She has made a home and a business here for her new son and is an inspiration to everyone that crosses paths with her! I'm glad that me and Kayleigh have her in our lives! So much so, that we don't want to let her go!" I watch Kayleigh hand her dad a little box, as a path from the stage to me opens up.

I immediately feel the heat rise in my cheeks as I see Sylvia at the front cradling Kian in her arms.

"Molly! You know how much I love you, so I am not going to be like a broken record. I do want you to know that I want you in my life 24/7. I want to wake up with you and fall asleep beside you. I want us to share the responsibility of the kids. You love my daughter just as much as I love your son and I'm sick of saying my daughter and your son. They're our kids!"

Kayleigh runs up to me and wraps her arms around me. I follow her lead and wrap my arms around her petite frame. "Molly? Will you do me the honor of becoming my wife?" Greg bent down on one knee on the stage.

Kayleigh looks up at me as I feel the tears roll down my cheeks. I am an emotional wreck just hearing Greg confess his love to me in front of everyone.

It's so quiet in here that you could literally hear a pin drop. Everyone wants to hear my answer.

I take Kayleigh's hand and walk slowly up to the stage. "You can stand up now daddy. You look kind of silly," she said.

The whole room is in hysterics. It is amazing how kids can just speak and not even realize how funny they are.

Greg ruffles her hair and stands up to tower over me. Even with heals on, I'm still a good few inches shorter than the love of my life. "What do you say, Molly?" asked Greg one last time, as he rests his hand on my cheek.

"I love you, Greg. I can't believe I didn't see this coming. I will marry you."

His big arms wrap around me as everyone cheers. Kayleigh goes to stand beside Sylvia, as Greg's lips caress mine.

I can't believe this is happening. "You have just made me the happiest man alive, Molly!"

We walk off the stage, hand in hand. Before anyone comes near us, Greg takes Kian from Sylvia's arms.

Our families are first in line to give us their best wishes. Greg's mum is so excited for us.

"Congratulations to you both," said my dad, shaking Greg's hand. "I hope you will both be very happy together."

"Thank you, dad." I place a kiss on his cheek but I have a feeling that something is wrong. I'm not bringing it up now, but I will make a point to ask him tonight.

I'm too damn happy to care about anything else.

***

As my opening event was drawing to a close, I said my goodbye's to a lot of new clients. Today has been such a success and now I hope to carry on the party with my family and friends.

I want to shout from the rooftops that I'm marrying Greg. I have laughed and smiled so much this afternoon, that I got cramps in my cheeks.

"Thank you for inviting us today, Molly. We really look forward to doing business with you." I knew this lady's name but I was struggling to remember.

"Aw, thank you. It has been lovely meeting you."

A strong pair of arms wrap around my waist and I relax into the strong embrace that I know belongs to my Greg.

"This is how I love to see you," Greg whispers into my ear, as he places soft kisses on my neck.

"What would that be? Tired, all smiled out, and missing your company?" I joked, trying to keep the mood going.

"I missed you too, but I meant happy, gorgeous, and relaxed."

"I feel happy all thanks to you."

"I don't know what I did to make you happy." I slap his arm as I giggled.

"I do hope we don't end up with a dozen of these little..." my dad trails off and looks up at Sylvia as she approaches us.

My motherly instinct kicks in and I take my son into my arms. "Little what, dad?"

I feel the hurt and anger rise inside me, because I know that my dad hasn't taken to Kian because of his disability.

"Little bambinos. I was going to say."

"I don't know what your problem is with my son but if you can't accept that he has Down's Syndrome, then you know what you can do!" I snapped.

"Molly..."

"Don't Molly me," I kissed Kian's tiny head as it rested on my chest. "I was leaving this until tonight but you just had to say something now. This is my son's home and he is going to grow up knowing that this is his safe haven. He's going to hear things when he gets older, but here he will be loved and taught the true meaning of love and family. He will not hear any hurtful things here. I expected more from you, dad."

"You took it the wrong way, Molly."

"That's why you've seen your grandson once since he was born." It was written all over his face.

"You're not close to me now, Molly."

"That's why you haven't held him or even looked at him today."

"He doesn't know me. He's comfortable with Greg and Sylvia."

"He's also comfortable with Greg's family!" I shouted, without realizing that there was a crowd around us now. "He's never going to know you, if you don't make an effort," I said, more calmly

"Can we talk about this later at the house?" asked my dad.

"I have nothing left to say to you. My mum will be turning in her grave with the way you have behaved."

"That isn't fair, Molly."

"Fair? I'll tell you what isn't fair! You're treating your grandson like he has the plague!"

"I set up his trust fund when he was born." I had to laugh as I looked down at my tiny son cuddled into my chest with not a care in the world.

"He doesn't need money! He needs love and support!" I quickly turned away from my dad and about died when I saw my ex Bradley, leaning against the doorframe looking very smug.

"What are you doing here?" I snapped.

"That's a very nice welcome, Molly. Am I not allowed to see my son?"

"Don't make me laugh! You gave up all rights to your son the moment you told me to get an abortion!" I wanted this opening party to go well, but I should have known that something would have happened to spoil things.

"When your dad told me that you stupidly kept it, I needed to see for myself." I turned back to look at my dad and his head was lowered so he couldn't look me in the eye.

"Well, now that you have seen for yourself, you can get off of my property!" I watched him look around the barn taking in everything like a child in a sweetie shop.

"I see you've landed on your feet here."

"I haven't landed on anything. It's called hard work. It is called bringing up a child."

Bradley walking up to me and Kian made my blood run cold. I just wanted Greg to claim his position beside me, but before I could see where he was, my brother Grey was there.

"You've got two minutes to get away from my sister and nephew or I'll kick you out of here myself!" exclaimed Grey.

I was proud of my brother for doing this, because we haven't been that close lately. It was nice to know if I had a problem, he would stand up and help me.

"Don't worry. I'll be leaving after I say what I came here to say."

I turned and handed Kian back to Sylvia, before my baby boy picked up on my emotions. "I don't want anything to do with any baby, let alone a baby that I can't love."

"You had a wasted trip, because you were never included in his life," said my brother, as I placed my hand on his arm to keep him calm.

I don't know where my courage came from but I walked right up to the asshole that I called a sperm donor and slapped him across the face.

"Don't you ever come back here! That man over there has been more of a father to my son, than you ever could! You make me sick! You are a worthless piece of shit that doesn't deserve air to breathe! Does it make you feel like a big man coming out here?"

"Since when did you get a set of balls?" He teased me, as he rubbed his red cheek.

"Since I had a child with special needs! Since I have to protect him from people like you!"

"Pfft!" He laughed in my face like this was one big joke to him. Something inside of me snapped and I flew at the worthless arse hole. I gave him everything I had until I felt Greg wrap himself around me and remove me from the situation.

"He isn't worth it, babe," said Greg, placing a kiss on the top of my head.

"You should listen to lover boy. He should get you under control." I went to pull out of Greg's arms but he had me safely held back out of the way. "It will only be so long before he gets fed up of looking at you and your sprog." Greg handed me over to my brother, but I didn't want him in the middle of this mess.

Greg punched the arse hole for all he was worth.

"You ever speak about my fiancé or step-son like that again, and it will be more than a broken nose that you leave here with," explained Greg calmly into this prick's face.

"You are welcome to them! I hope that bitch can give you more than she gave me!"

Another punch and Bradley fell against the wall.

Greg had him pinned up against the wall and I urged my brother to stop him. He let me go, but he stood back in case Greg needed him.

"I warned you! I warned you to keep your mouth shut! Now this is what is going to happen. You're going to get the hell out of here and never come back. You step one foot near Molly or Kian and you they will be feeding you through a tube! Do I make myself clear?"

"Perfectly," Bradley squeaked out.

Greg threw him out the door and we all watched as he landed on the ground. "One last thing. When Molly gets her solicitor to draw up the papers, you will sign any rights of the baby over to Molly. You will let me and Molly give him a life he deserves."

"Fine!"

Greg walked back to me and took me in his arms. I couldn't control my tears as I sobbed into his chest.

"We're sorry about this everyone. Please don't hold this against my sister. She is bloody good at what she does," said my brother.

"He's lucky that Greg let him off lightly. He deserved more. Much more," said one of the bystanders.

"I am so sorry everyone, but I need to get out of here. Please finish your drinks or continue with the party." I managed to hold back any more tears until I took Kian from Sylvia and took Kayleigh's hand in mine.

We made our way out of the barn and back up toward the house. I knew that Greg would be right behind us, so I never stopped to look back.

I should have listened to my nerves this morning. I knew that something was going to happen but I couldn't put my finger on it. Usually when I get a gut feeling, I am right. I let my guard down today and that was the price I had to pay.

***

Today has been one of those days that feels like one big nightmare. In many ways it had many high moments that I would never forget.

Just lying on top of the bed with the pile of client contracts, makes me very proud at how far I have come.

Knowing that I have a fiancé makes my body come alive in ways that I have never felt before.

Then when I think about the low moments of today, Bradley and his show just makes me so angry. Even now, a few hours after, I could still kill him.

Then there was my dad. Although he apologized before he went back to Sylvia's B&B, it still didn't make everything all right between us.

I feel like an emotional wreck as I lay here reliving my day. Kian and Kayleigh are tucked up in bed, so I know they won't see me upset but I know that Greg will know right away when he comes back from the shower. It was like he had some detector inside of him that could pick up on my thoughts and feelings.

"Molly," said Greg, stopping at the door with just a towel around him. He looks so handsome. So handsome that he always takes my breath away. "What is wrong, babe?"

Greg crossed the room and sat on the side of the bed wrapping me in his arms.

We were like Yin and Yang. We fit perfectly together whenever we come together as one. "Is this about today?"

All I could do was nod my head into his chest. I knew that he would need to be looking into my eyes when he spoke to me. "Don't listen to anything that waste of space said. We are a family now and I'll take care of you both. Not that you need me, but I want to be here with you both. He won't be back here."

"What do you see when you look at Kian?" I asked, dreading what he was going to say, because I know when he is lying.

"Molly. When I look into Kian's eyes and he smiles at me like I am his whole world, it melts my heart. He might not be my blood Molly, but he is mine. If you let me, I will bring him up as my own. I will even adopt him. I love you both. Nothing, I mean nothing is going to change that."

"Why do people have to see Down's Syndrome as a bad thing? He's human. He loves and shares feelings just like us all."

I had strong feelings about the way people treat special needs. I would fight to the end of the earth for anyone with Down's syndrome.

"Some people are just ignorant. He won't have to worry about people not loving him. Everyone who enters your house, or mine, will treat him with love and respect. That, I will make sure."

"*Our* house," I said, placing my hand on Greg's bare chest.

"What?"

"You said my house or your house, but this is our house. I want you and Kayleigh to move in here with me and Kian. You're here anyway, so it's just making it official."

"If this is what you want."

"Of course, it is. Let's start a new life together."

We both had smiles on our faces and love in our eyes. Where tonight was going to lead was obvious, when Greg's lips caressed mine. The love and passion was like electricity sparking through both of us as Greg laid me down on the bed.

Making love with Greg is beautiful.

I now have everything I ever wanted in life. A house. A business. A life. A family. A husband.

Now life was perfect. My country escape has become the best move that I have ever made.

THE END

How To Contact The Author

Find us on Facebook

www.facebook.com/authorkmlowe

@KMLOWE86

www.goodreads.com/KMLOWE

Please get in contact with me, because I really do like talking to my readers.

Other Work By KM Lowe

The Beautiful Life Trilogy

Book 1 - The Smile

Book 2 - The Smile - New Beginnings

Book 3 - The Smile - Forever After

Romance

It Was Meant To Be

A Country Escape

Music Play List

Skerryvore - Caledonia

Skerryvore - We're The Lucky Ones

Skerryvore - Hold Me Tonight

Skerryvore - The Last Time

Jess Glynn - Take Me home

Jess Glynn - Don't Be So Hard On Yourself

Jess Glynn - Ain't Got Far To Go

Savage Garden - Truly Madly Deeply

Shane Filan - Knee Deep In My Heart

Shane Filan - Everything To Me

James Bay - Let It Go

James Bay - Hold Back The River

A Country Escape

Molly has had a rough couple of years. Losing her mum is one thing, but getting out of a bad relationship to realize that she is pregnant is another.

Molly decides that in order to get her life back on track, she needs to move away from her family home in Aberdeen, to a small country village in Stirling. Little did she know that this move was going to be the best thing she ever did.

Molly's new home and business plans all work out nicely. Her offer on Ethel's Farm is accepted and her business plans get the go ahead. Greg Macintosh helps her get everything sorted. Their friendship blossoms but Molly can't accept her feelings for him. She thinks that because she has a baby on the way, she has to live the rest of her life as a single mum.

A trip to Aviemore in December is eventful to say the least. Molly walks away from her chance of happiness. That is until things take a turn and Molly and Greg are thrown into the arms of one another to get through a tricky situation.

Can their friendship progress to something else, or do they end up going their own separate ways?

61878327R00124

Made in the USA
Charleston, SC
30 September 2016